SSAT MIDDLE LEVEL MATH TUTOR

Everything You Need to Help Achieve an Excellent Score

By

Reza Nazari

&

Ava Ross

About Effortless Math Education

Effortless Math Education operates the www.effortlessmath.com website, which prepares and publishes Test prep and Mathematics learning resources. Effortless Math authors' team strives to prepare and publish the best quality Mathematics learning resources to make learning Math easier for all. We Help Students Learn to Love Mathematics.

Copyright © 2023
Effortless Math

All inquiries should be addressed to:
info@effortlessMath.com
www.EffortlessMath.com

ISBN: 978-1-64612-849-5

Published by: **Effortless Math Education**

for Online Math Practice Visit www.EffortlessMath.com

SSAT MIDDLE LEVEL MATH TUTOR

All the Tools You Need to Succeed on the SSAT Middle Level Math test 2023!

Feeling anxious about the SSAT Middle Level? Not sure your math skills are up to the task? Don't worry, *SSAT Middle Level Math Tutor* has you covered!

Focusing on proven test-taking strategies, easy-to-understand math principles, and professional guidance, *SSAT Middle Level Math Tutor* is your comprehensive study guide for the SSAT Middle Level Math test!

Each chapter includes a study-guide formatted review and quizzes to check your comprehension on the topics covered. With this self-study guide, it's like having your own tutor for a fraction of the cost!

What does the SSAT Middle Level Math Tutor offer?

- Content 100% aligned with the 2023 SSAT Middle Level test

- **Step-by-Step guides** to all SSAT Middle Level Math concepts and topics covered in the 2023 test

- **Over 500 additional SSAT Middle Level math practice questions** featuring multiple-choice and grid-in formats with answers grouped by topic, so you can focus on your weak areas

- Abundant Math skill-building exercises to help test-takers approach different question types that might be unfamiliar to them

- **2 full-length practice tests** (featuring new question types) with detailed answers.

The surest way to succeed on the SSAT Middle Level Math Test is with intensive practice in every math topic tested—and that's what exactly what you'll get! With the SSAT Middle Level Math Tutor, you'll have everything you need to ace the SSAT Middle Level right in your hands. *Start studying today!*

About the Author

Reza Nazari is the author of more than 100 Math learning books including:

- ❖ **Math and Critical Thinking Challenges:** For the Middle and High School Student
- ❖ **ACT Math in 30 Days**
- ❖ **ASVAB Math Workbook**
- ❖ **Effortless Math Education Workbooks**
- ❖ **and many more Mathematics books**

Reza is also an experienced Math instructor and a test–prep expert who has been tutoring students since 2008. Reza is the founder of Effortless Math Education, a tutoring company that has helped many students raise their standardized test scores—and attend the colleges of their dreams. Reza provides an individualized custom learning plan and the personalized attention that makes a difference in how students view math.

You can contact Reza via email at:
reza@EffortlessMath.com

Find Reza's professional profile at:
goo.gl/zoC9rJ

Contents

CHAPTER 1:

FRACTIONS AND MIXED NUMBERS

Math Topics that you'll learn in this chapter:

▶ Simplifying Fractions

▶ Adding and Subtracting Fractions

▶ Multiplying and Dividing Fractions

▶ Adding Mixed Numbers

▶ Subtracting Mixed Numbers

▶ Multiplying Mixed Numbers

▶ Dividing Mixed Numbers

SIMPLIFYING FRACTIONS

☑ A fraction contains two numbers separated by a bar between them. The bottom number, called the denominator, is the total number of equally divided portions in one whole. The top number, called the numerator, is how many portions you have. And the bar represents the operation of division.

☑ Simplifying a fraction means reducing it to the lowest terms. To simplify a fraction, evenly divide both the top and bottom of the fraction by $2, 3, 5, 7$, etc.

☑ Continue until you can't go any further.

Examples:

Example 1. Simplify $\frac{12}{30}$

Solution: To simplify $\frac{12}{30}$, find a number that both 12 and 30 are divisible by. Both are divisible by 6. Then: $\frac{12}{30} = \frac{12 \div 6}{30 \div 6} = \frac{2}{5}$

Example 2. Simplify $\frac{64}{80}$

Solution: To simplify $\frac{64}{80}$, find a number that both 64 and 80 are divisible by. Both are divisible by 8 and 16. Then: $\frac{64}{80} = \frac{64 \div 8}{80 \div 8} = \frac{8}{10}$, 8 and 10 are divisible by 2, then: $\frac{8}{10} = \frac{4}{5}$ or $\frac{64}{80} = \frac{64 \div 16}{80 \div 16} = \frac{4}{5}$

Example 3. Simplify $\frac{20}{60}$

Solution: To simplify $\frac{20}{60}$, find a number that both 20 and 60 are divisible by. Both are divisible by 20, then: $\frac{20}{60} = \frac{20 \div 20}{60 \div 20} = \frac{1}{3}$

ADDING AND SUBTRACTING FRACTIONS

☑ For "like" fractions (fractions with the same denominator), add or subtract the numerators (top numbers) and write the answer over the common denominator (bottom numbers).

☑ Adding and Subtracting fractions with the same denominator:

$$\frac{a}{b} + \frac{c}{b} = \frac{a+c}{b} \qquad \frac{a}{b} - \frac{c}{b} = \frac{a-c}{b}$$

☑ Find equivalent fractions with the same denominator before you can add or subtract fractions with different denominators.

☑ Adding and Subtracting fractions with different denominators:

$$\frac{a}{b} + \frac{c}{d} = \frac{ad+bc}{bd} \qquad \frac{a}{b} - \frac{c}{d} = \frac{ad-bc}{bd}$$

Examples:

Example 1. Find the sum. $\frac{3}{4} + \frac{1}{3} =$

Solution: These two fractions are "unlike" fractions. (they have different denominators). Use this formula: $\frac{a}{b} + \frac{c}{d} = \frac{ad+cb}{bd}$

Then: $\frac{3}{4} + \frac{1}{3} = \frac{(3)(3)+(4)(1)}{4 \times 3} = \frac{9+4}{12} = \frac{13}{12}$

Example 2. Find the difference. $\frac{4}{5} - \frac{3}{7} =$

Solution: For "unlike" fractions, find equivalent fractions with the same denominator before you can add or subtract fractions with different denominators. Use this formula:

$\frac{a}{b} - \frac{c}{d} = \frac{ad-bc}{bd}$

$\frac{4}{5} - \frac{3}{7} = \frac{(4)(7)-(3)(5)}{5 \times 7} = \frac{28-15}{35} = \frac{13}{35}$

MULTIPLYING AND DIVIDING FRACTIONS

- ☑ Multiplying fractions: multiply the top numbers and multiply the bottom numbers. Simplify if necessary. $\quad \frac{a}{b} \times \frac{c}{d} = \frac{a \times c}{b \times d}$

- ☑ Dividing fractions: Keep, Change, Flip

- ☑ Keep the first fraction, change the division sign to multiplication, and flip the numerator and denominator of the second fraction. Then, solve!

$$\frac{a}{b} \div \frac{c}{d} = \frac{a}{b} \times \frac{d}{c} = \frac{a \times d}{b \times c}$$

Examples:

Example 1. Multiply. $\frac{5}{8} \times \frac{2}{3} =$

Solution: Multiply the top numbers and multiply the bottom numbers. $\frac{5}{8} \times \frac{2}{3} = \frac{5 \times 2}{8 \times 3} = \frac{10}{24}$, simplify: $\frac{10}{24} = \frac{10 \div 2}{24 \div 2} = \frac{5}{12}$

Example 2. Solve. $\frac{1}{3} \div \frac{4}{7} =$

Solution: Keep the first fraction, change the division sign to multiplication, and flip the numerator and denominator of the second fraction.
Then: $\frac{1}{3} \div \frac{4}{7} = \frac{1}{3} \times \frac{7}{4} = \frac{1 \times 7}{3 \times 4} = \frac{7}{12}$

Example 3. Calculate. $\frac{3}{5} \times \frac{2}{3} =$

Solution: Multiply the top numbers and multiply the bottom numbers. $\frac{3}{5} \times \frac{2}{3} = \frac{3 \times 2}{5 \times 3} = \frac{6}{15}$, simplify: $\frac{6}{15} = \frac{6 \div 3}{15 \div 3} = \frac{2}{5}$

Example 4. Solve. $\frac{1}{4} \div \frac{5}{6} =$

Solution: Keep the first fraction, change the division sign to multiplication, and flip the numerator and denominator of the second fraction.
Then: $\frac{1}{4} \div \frac{5}{6} = \frac{1}{4} \times \frac{6}{5} = \frac{1 \times 6}{4 \times 5} = \frac{6}{20}$, simplify: $\frac{6}{20} = \frac{6 \div 2}{20 \div 2} = \frac{3}{10}$

ADDING MIXED NUMBERS

Use the following steps for adding mixed numbers:

- ☑ Add whole numbers of the mixed numbers.

- ☑ Add the fractions of the mixed numbers.

- ☑ Find the Least Common Denominator (LCD) if necessary.

- ☑ Add whole numbers and fractions.

- ☑ Write your answer in lowest terms.

Examples:

Example 1. Add mixed numbers. $3\frac{1}{3} + 1\frac{4}{5} =$

Solution: Let's rewriting our equation with parts separated, $3\frac{1}{3} + 1\frac{4}{5} = 3 + \frac{1}{3} + 1 + \frac{4}{5}$. Now, add whole number parts: $3 + 1 = 4$

Add the fraction parts $\frac{1}{3} + \frac{4}{5}$. Rewrite to solve with the equivalent fractions. $\frac{1}{3} + \frac{4}{5} = \frac{5}{15} + \frac{12}{15} = \frac{17}{15}$. The answer is an improper fraction (numerator is bigger than denominator). Convert the improper fraction into a mixed number: $\frac{17}{15} = 1\frac{2}{15}$. Now, combine the whole and fraction parts: $4 + 1\frac{2}{15} = 5\frac{2}{15}$

Example 2. Find the sum. $1\frac{2}{5} + 2\frac{1}{2} =$

Solution: Rewriting our equation with parts separated, $1 + \frac{2}{5} + 2 + \frac{1}{2}$. Add the whole number parts:

$1 + 2 = 3$. Add the fraction parts: $\frac{2}{5} + \frac{1}{2} = \frac{4}{10} + \frac{5}{10} = \frac{9}{10}$

Now, combine the whole and fraction parts: $3 + \frac{9}{10} = 3\frac{9}{10}$

SUBTRACT MIXED NUMBERS

Use these steps for subtracting mixed numbers.

☑ Convert mixed numbers into improper fractions. $a\frac{c}{b} = \frac{ab+c}{b}$

☑ Find equivalent fractions with the same denominator for unlike fractions. (fractions with different denominators)

☑ Subtract the second fraction from the first one. $\frac{a}{b} - \frac{c}{d} = \frac{ad-bc}{bd}$

☑ Write your answer in lowest terms.

☑ If the answer is an improper fraction, convert it into a mixed number.

Examples:

Example 1. Subtract. $3\frac{4}{5} - 1\frac{3}{4} =$

Solution: Convert mixed numbers into fractions: $3\frac{4}{5} = \frac{3\times5+4}{5} = \frac{19}{5}$ and $1\frac{3}{4} = \frac{1\times4+3}{4} = \frac{7}{4}$

These two fractions are "unlike" fractions. (they have different denominators). Find equivalent fractions with the same denominator. Use this formula: $\frac{a}{b} - \frac{c}{d} = \frac{ad-bc}{bd}$

$\frac{19}{5} - \frac{7}{4} = \frac{(19)(4)-(5)(7)}{5\times4} = \frac{76-35}{20} = \frac{41}{20}$, the answer is an improper fraction, convert it into a mixed number. $\frac{41}{20} = 2\frac{1}{20}$

Example 2. Subtract. $4\frac{3}{8} - 1\frac{1}{2} =$

Solution: Convert mixed numbers into fractions: $4\frac{3}{8} = \frac{4\times8+3}{8} = \frac{35}{8}$ and $1\frac{1}{2} = \frac{1\times2+1}{4} = \frac{3}{2}$

Find equivalent fractions: $\frac{3}{2} = \frac{12}{8}$. Then: $4\frac{3}{8} - 1\frac{1}{2} = \frac{35}{8} - \frac{12}{8} = \frac{23}{8}$

The answer is an improper fraction, convert it into a mixed number.

$$\frac{23}{8} = 2\frac{7}{8}$$

MULTIPLYING MIXED NUMBERS

Use the following steps for multiplying mixed numbers:

☑ Convert the mixed numbers into fractions. $a\frac{c}{b} = a + \frac{c}{b} = \frac{ab+c}{b}$

☑ Multiply fractions. $\frac{a}{b} \times \frac{c}{d} = \frac{a \times c}{b \times d}$

☑ Write your answer in lowest terms.

☑ If the answer is an improper fraction (numerator is bigger than denominator), convert it into a mixed number.

Examples:

Example 1. Multiply. $3\frac{1}{3} \times 4\frac{1}{6} =$

Solution: Convert mixed numbers into fractions, $3\frac{1}{3} = \frac{3 \times 3 + 1}{3} = \frac{10}{3}$ and $4\frac{1}{6} = \frac{4 \times 6 + 1}{6} = \frac{25}{6}$

Apply the fractions rule for multiplication, $\frac{10}{3} \times \frac{25}{6} = \frac{10 \times 25}{3 \times 6} = \frac{250}{18}$

The answer is an improper fraction. Convert it into a mixed number. $\frac{250}{18} = 13\frac{8}{9}$

Example 2. Multiply. $2\frac{1}{2} \times 3\frac{2}{3} =$

Solution: Converting mixed numbers into fractions, $2\frac{1}{2} \times 3\frac{2}{3} = \frac{5}{2} \times \frac{11}{3}$

Apply the fractions rule for multiplication, $\frac{5}{2} \times \frac{11}{3} = \frac{5 \times 11}{2 \times 3} = \frac{55}{6} = 9\frac{1}{6}$

Example 3. Multiply mixed numbers. $2\frac{1}{3} \times 2\frac{1}{2} =$

Solution: Converting mixed numbers to fractions, $2\frac{1}{3} = \frac{7}{3}$ and $2\frac{1}{2} = \frac{5}{2}$.
Multiply two fractions:

$$\frac{7}{3} \times \frac{5}{2} = \frac{7 \times 5}{3 \times 2} = \frac{35}{6} = 5\frac{5}{6}$$

DIVIDING MIXED NUMBERS

Use the following steps for dividing mixed numbers:

☑ Convert the mixed numbers into fractions. $a\frac{c}{b} = a + \frac{c}{b} = \frac{ab+c}{b}$

☑ Divide fractions: Keep, Change, Flip: Keep the first fraction, change the division sign to multiplication, and flip the numerator and denominator of the second fraction. Then, solve! $\frac{a}{b} \div \frac{c}{d} = \frac{a}{b} \times \frac{d}{c} = \frac{a \times d}{b \times c}$

☑ Write your answer in lowest terms.

☑ If the answer is an improper fraction (numerator is bigger than denominator), convert it into a mixed number.

Examples:

Example 1. Solve. $3\frac{2}{3} \div 2\frac{1}{2}$

Solution: Convert mixed numbers into fractions: $3\frac{2}{3} = \frac{3\times3+2}{3} = \frac{11}{3}$ and $2\frac{1}{2} = \frac{2\times2+1}{2} = \frac{5}{2}$

Keep, Change, Flip: $\frac{11}{3} \div \frac{5}{2} = \frac{11}{3} \times \frac{2}{5} = \frac{11\times2}{3\times5} = \frac{22}{15}$. The answer is an improper fraction. Convert it into a mixed number: $\frac{22}{15} = 1\frac{7}{15}$

Example 2. Solve. $3\frac{4}{5} \div 1\frac{5}{6}$

Solution: Convert mixed numbers to fractions, then solve:

$3\frac{4}{5} \div 1\frac{5}{6} = \frac{19}{5} \div \frac{11}{6} = \frac{19}{5} \times \frac{6}{11} = \frac{114}{55} = 2\frac{4}{55}$

Example 3. Solve. $2\frac{2}{7} \div 2\frac{3}{5}$

Solution: Converting mixed numbers to fractions: $3\frac{4}{5} \div 1\frac{5}{6} = \frac{16}{7} \div \frac{13}{5}$

Keep, Change, Flip: $\frac{16}{7} \div \frac{13}{5} = \frac{16}{7} \times \frac{5}{13} = \frac{16\times5}{7\times13} = \frac{80}{91}$

CHAPTER 1: PRACTICES

✎ Simplify each fraction.

1) $\dfrac{16}{24} =$

2) $\dfrac{28}{70} =$

3) $\dfrac{30}{105} =$

4) $\dfrac{40}{35} =$

5) $\dfrac{48}{56} =$

6) $\dfrac{6}{120} =$

7) $\dfrac{15}{100} =$

8) $\dfrac{45}{54} =$

✎ Find the sum or difference.

9) $\dfrac{4}{12} + \dfrac{3}{12} =$

10) $\dfrac{5}{4} + \dfrac{1}{12} =$

11) $\dfrac{3}{6} + \dfrac{2}{5} =$

12) $\dfrac{8}{25} - \dfrac{3}{25} =$

13) $\dfrac{5}{3} - \dfrac{2}{9} =$

14) $\dfrac{3}{2} - \dfrac{3}{4} =$

15) $\dfrac{4}{3} - \dfrac{6}{5} =$

16) $\dfrac{5}{12} + \dfrac{3}{5} =$

✎ Find the products or quotients.

17) $\dfrac{9}{5} \div \dfrac{3}{2} =$

18) $\dfrac{8}{7} \div \dfrac{4}{3} =$

19) $\dfrac{6}{4} \times \dfrac{8}{5} =$

20) $\dfrac{7}{2} \times \dfrac{4}{9} =$

✎ Find the sum.

21) $2\dfrac{1}{3} + 1\dfrac{4}{5} =$

22) $4\dfrac{3}{7} + 3\dfrac{3}{4} =$

23) $2\dfrac{3}{4} + 3\dfrac{1}{3} =$

24) $1\dfrac{1}{4} + 3\dfrac{1}{2} =$

25) $2\dfrac{5}{7} + 2\dfrac{1}{3} =$

26) $4\dfrac{2}{9} + 2\dfrac{1}{2} =$

✎ **Find the difference.**

27) $4\frac{2}{9} - 3\frac{1}{7} =$

28) $3\frac{3}{4} - 2\frac{1}{8} =$

29) $3\frac{2}{7} - 2\frac{4}{9} =$

30) $8\frac{3}{4} - 2\frac{1}{8} =$

31) $5\frac{5}{6} - 3\frac{1}{24} =$

32) $7\frac{3}{10} - 4\frac{4}{5} =$

33) $8\frac{1}{6} - 3\frac{2}{3} =$

34) $14\frac{9}{10} - 8\frac{4}{5} =$

✎ **Find the products.**

35) $2\frac{1}{9} \times 2\frac{5}{6} =$

36) $2\frac{3}{4} \times 4\frac{1}{9} =$

37) $1\frac{2}{7} \times 1\frac{5}{6} =$

38) $3\frac{2}{9} \times 1\frac{6}{5} =$

39) $3\frac{2}{3} \times 2\frac{3}{5} =$

40) $2\frac{5}{6} \times 3\frac{1}{9} =$

41) $3\frac{4}{5} \times 1\frac{1}{6} =$

42) $4\frac{1}{5} \times 1\frac{2}{7} =$

✎ **Solve.**

43) $8\frac{3}{4} \div 4\frac{1}{3} =$

44) $4\frac{2}{5} \div 1\frac{2}{9} =$

45) $6\frac{1}{2} \div 2\frac{1}{3} =$

46) $7\frac{1}{6} \div 3\frac{4}{9} =$

47) $2\frac{1}{4} \div 1\frac{1}{8} =$

48) $3\frac{2}{5} \div 1\frac{1}{10} =$

49) $4\frac{1}{2} \div 2\frac{2}{3} =$

50) $11\frac{1}{3} \div 2\frac{2}{9} =$

CHAPTER 1: ANSWERS

1) $\dfrac{2}{3}$

2) $\dfrac{2}{5}$

3) $\dfrac{2}{7}$

4) $\dfrac{8}{7}$

5) $\dfrac{6}{7}$

6) $\dfrac{1}{20}$

7) $\dfrac{3}{20}$

8) $\dfrac{5}{6}$

9) $\dfrac{7}{12}$

10) $\dfrac{4}{3}$

11) $\dfrac{9}{10}$

12) $\dfrac{1}{5}$

13) $\dfrac{13}{9} = 1\dfrac{4}{9}$

14) $\dfrac{3}{4}$

15) $\dfrac{2}{15}$

16) $\dfrac{61}{60} = 1\dfrac{1}{60}$

17) $\dfrac{6}{5}$

18) $\dfrac{6}{7}$

19) $\dfrac{12}{5} = 2\dfrac{2}{5}$

20) $\dfrac{14}{9} = 1\dfrac{5}{9}$

21) $4\dfrac{2}{15}$

22) $8\dfrac{5}{28}$

23) $6\dfrac{1}{12}$

24) $4\dfrac{3}{4}$

25) $5\dfrac{1}{21}$

26) $6\dfrac{13}{18}$

27) $1\dfrac{5}{63}$

28) $1\dfrac{5}{8}$

29) $\dfrac{53}{63}$

30) $6\dfrac{5}{8}$

31) $2\dfrac{19}{24}$

32) $2\dfrac{1}{2}$

33) $4\dfrac{1}{2}$

34) $6\dfrac{1}{10}$

35) $5\dfrac{53}{54}$

36) $11\dfrac{11}{63}$

37) $2\dfrac{5}{14}$

38) $7\dfrac{4}{45}$

39) $9\dfrac{18}{15}$

40) $8\dfrac{22}{27}$

41) $4\dfrac{13}{30}$

42) $5\dfrac{2}{5}$

43) $2\dfrac{1}{52}$

44) $3\dfrac{3}{5}$

45) $2\dfrac{11}{14}$

46) $2\dfrac{5}{62}$

47) 2

48) $3\dfrac{1}{11}$

49) $1\dfrac{11}{16}$

50) $5\dfrac{1}{10}$

CHAPTER 2:

DECIMALS

Math Topics that you'll learn in this chapter:

▶ Comparing Decimals

▶ Rounding Decimals

▶ Adding and Subtracting Decimals

▶ Multiplying and Dividing Decimals

COMPARING DECIMALS

☑ A decimal is a fraction written in a special form. For example, instead of writing $\frac{1}{2}$ you can write 0.5

☑ A Decimal Number contains a Decimal Point. It separates the whole number part from the fractional part of a decimal number.

☑ Let's review decimal place values: Example: **53.9861**

5: tens	3: ones	9: tenths
8: hundredths	6: thousandths	1: tens thousandths

☑ To compare decimals, compare each digit of two decimals in the same place value. Start from left. Compare hundreds, tens, ones, tenth, hundredth, etc.

☑ To compare numbers, use these symbols:

Equal to =,	Less than <,	Greater than >
Greater than or equal ≥,	Less than or equal ≤	

Examples:

Example 1. Compare 0.60 and 0.06.

Solution: 0.60 *is greater than* 0.06, because the tenth place of 0.60 is 6, but the tenth place of 0.06 is zero. Then: 0.60 > 0.06

Example 2. Compare 0.0815 and 0.815.

Solution: 0.815 *is greater than* 0.0815, because the tenth place of 0.815 is 8, but the tenth place of 0.0815 is zero. Then: 0.0815 < 0.815

ROUNDING DECIMALS

- Ø We can round decimals to a certain accuracy or number of decimal places. This is used to make calculations easier to do and results easier to understand when exact values are not too important.

- Ø First, you'll need to remember your place values: For example: **12.4869**

  1: tens   2: ones   4: tenths

  8: hundredths   6: thousandths   9: tens thousandths

- Ø To round a decimal, first find the place value you'll round to.

- Ø Find the digit to the right of the place value you're rounding to. If it is 5 or bigger, add 1 to the place value you're rounding to and remove all digits on its right side. If the digit to the right of the place value is less than 5, keep the place value and remove all digits on the right.

Examples:

Example 1. Round 1.9278 to the thousandth place value.

Solution: First, look at the next place value to the right, (tens thousandths). It's 8 and it is greater than 5. Thus add 1 to the digit in the thousandth place. The thousandth place is 7. $\rightarrow 7 + 1 = 8$, then,
The answer is 1.928

Example 2. Round 9.4126 to the nearest hundredth.

Solution: First, look at the digit to the right of hundredth (thousandths place value). It's 2 and it is less than 5, thus remove all the digits to the right of hundredth place. Then, the answer is 9.41

ADDING AND SUBTRACTING DECIMALS

☑ Line up the decimal numbers.

☑ Add zeros to have the same number of digits for both numbers if necessary.

☑ Remember your place values: For example: 73.5196

7: tens	3: ones	5: tenths
1: hundredths	9: thousandths	6: tens thousandths

☑ Add or subtract using column addition or subtraction.

Examples:

Example 1. Add. $1.8 + 3.12$

Solution: First, line up the numbers: $\begin{array}{r} 1.8 \\ + 3.12 \\ \hline \end{array}$ → Add a zero to have the same number of digits for both numbers. $\begin{array}{r} 1.80 \\ + 3.12 \\ \hline \end{array}$ → Start with the hundredths place: $0 + 2 = 2$, $\begin{array}{r} 1.80 \\ + 3.12 \\ \hline 2 \end{array}$ → Continue with tenths place: $8 + 1 = 9$, $\begin{array}{r} 1.80 \\ + 3.12 \\ \hline .92 \end{array}$ → Add the ones place: $3 + 1 = 4$, $\begin{array}{r} 1.80 \\ + 3.12 \\ \hline 4.92 \end{array}$

Example 2. Find the difference. $3.67 - 2.23$

Solution: First, line up the numbers: $\begin{array}{r} 3.67 \\ - 2.23 \\ \hline \end{array}$ → Start with the hundredths place: $7 - 3 = 4$, $\begin{array}{r} 3.67 \\ - 2.23 \\ \hline 4 \end{array}$ → Continue with tenths place. $6 - 2 = 4$, $\begin{array}{r} 3.67 \\ - 2.23 \\ \hline .44 \end{array}$ → Subtract the ones place. $3 - 2 = 1$, $\begin{array}{r} 3.67 \\ - 2.23 \\ \hline 1.44 \end{array}$

MULTIPLYING AND DIVIDING DECIMALS

For multiplying decimals:

☑ Ignore the decimal point and set up and multiply the numbers as you do with whole numbers.

☑ Count the total number of decimal places in both of the factors.

☑ Place the decimal point in the product.

For dividing decimals:

☑ If the divisor is not a whole number, move the decimal point to the right to make it a whole number. Do the same for the dividend.

☑ Divide similar to whole numbers.

Examples:

Example 1. Find the product. $0.81 \times 0.32 =$

Solution: Set up and multiply the numbers as you do with whole numbers. Line up the numbers: $\begin{array}{r} 81 \\ \times 32 \\ \hline \end{array}$ → Start with the ones place then continue with other digits → $\begin{array}{r} 81 \\ \times 32 \\ \hline 2{,}592 \end{array}$. Count the total number of decimal places in both of the factors. There are four decimals digits. (two for each factor 0.81 and 0.32) Then: $0.81 \times 0.32 = 0.2592$

Example 2. Find the quotient. $1.60 \div 0.4 =$

Solution: The divisor is not a whole number. Multiply it by 10 to get 4: → $0.4 \times 10 = 4$
Do the same for the dividend to get 16. → $1.60 \times 10 = 1.6$
Now, divide $16 \div 4 = 4$. The answer is 4.

CHAPTER 2: PRACTICES

✎ Compare. Use >, =, and <

1) 0.55 ☐ 0.055

2) 0.34 ☐ 0.33

3) 0.66 ☐ 0.59

4) 2.650 ☐ 2.65

5) 2.34 ☐ 2.67

6) 2.46 ☐ 2.05

7) 0.16 ☐ 0.025

8) 5.05 ☐ 50.5

9) 1.020 ☐ 1.02

10) 3.022 ☐ 3.3

11) 1.400 ☐ 1.60

12) 3.44 ☐ 4.3

13) 0.380 ☐ 3.03

14) 2.081 ☐ 2.63

✎ Round each decimal to the nearest whole number.

15) 10.57

16) 4.8

17) 29.7

18) 32.58

19) 7.5

20) 8.87

21) 56.23

22) 6.39

23) 18.63

24) 25.56

25) 28.49

26) 12.67

27) 49.9

28) 17.77

29) 3.44

30) 55.56

✎ Find the sum or difference.

31) $25.31 + 56.37 =$

32) $78.32 - 65.10 =$

33) $65.80 + 14.26 =$

34) $90.24 - 53.81 =$

35) $76.41 - 49.27 =$

36) $45.39 + 17.86 =$

37) $56.02 + 30.60 =$

38) $67.01 - 28.40 =$

39) $75.14 - 25.96 =$

40) $37.52 + 13.50 =$

41) $84.71 - 54.18 =$

42) $24.12 + 29.84 =$

43) $50.59 - 46.25 =$

44) $63.13 + 21.14 =$

45) $45.23 - 35.17 =$

46) $18.02 + 30.40 =$

✎ Find the product or quotient.

47) $1.4 \times 3.2 =$

48) $8.2 \div 0.2 =$

49) 4.12×3.5

50) $6.8 \div 1.7 =$

51) $5.8 \times 0.5 =$

52) $1.54 \div 0.5 =$

53) $1.4 \times 3.2 =$

54) $5.8 \div 0.2 =$

55) $6.4 \times 7.3 =$

56) $0.3 \times 3.2 =$

57) $7.5 \times 5.6 =$

58) $45.6 \div 0.8 =$

59) $1.9 \times 5.8 =$

60) $6.74 \times 2.5 =$

61) $56.08 \div 0.2 =$

62) $36.2 \times 3.6 =$

CHAPTER 2: ANSWERS

1) >	22) 6	43) 4.34
2) >	23) 19	44) 84.27
3) >	24) 26	45) 10.06
4) =	25) 28	46) 48.42
5) <	26) 13	47) 4.48
6) >	27) 50	48) 41
7) >	28) 18	49) 14.42
8) <	29) 3	50) 4
9) =	30) 56	51) 2.9
10) <	31) 81.68	52) 3.08
11) <	32) 13.22	53) 4.48
12) <	33) 80.06	54) 29
13) <	34) 36.43	55) 46.72
14) <	35) 27.14	56) 0.96
15) 11	36) 63.25	57) 42
16) 5	37) 86.62	58) 57
17) 30	38) 38.61	59) 11.02
18) 33	39) 49.18	60) 16.85
19) 8	40) 51.02	61) 280.4
20) 9	41) 30.53	62) 130.32
21) 56	42) 53.96	

CHAPTER 3:

INTEGERS AND ORDER OF OPERATIONS

Math Topics that you'll learn in this chapter:

▶ Adding and Subtracting Integers

▶ Multiplying and Dividing Integers

▶ Order of Operations

▶ Integers and Absolute Value

ADDING AND SUBTRACTING INTEGERS

- ☑ Integers include zero, counting numbers, and the negative of the counting numbers. $\{\ldots, -3, -2, -1, 0, 1, 2, 3, \ldots\}$

- ☑ Add a positive integer by moving to the right on the number line. (you will get a bigger number)

- ☑ Add a negative integer by moving to the left on the number line. (you will get a smaller number)

- ☑ Subtract an integer by adding its opposite.

Examples:

Example 1. Solve. $(-4) - 5 =$

Solution: Keep the first number and convert the sign of the second number to its opposite. (change subtraction into addition. Then: $(-4) + 5 = 1$

Example 2. Solve. $11 + (8 - 19) =$

Solution: First, subtract the numbers in brackets, $8 - 19 = -11$. Then: $11 + (-11) = \rightarrow$ change addition into subtraction: $11 - 11 = 0$

Example 3. Solve. $5 - 14 - 3 =$

Solution: First, subtract the numbers in brackets, $-14 - 3 = -17$ Then: $5 - 17 = \rightarrow$ change subtraction into addition: $5 + 17 = 22$

Example 4. Solve. $10 + (-6 - 15) =$

Solution: First, subtract the numbers in brackets, $-6 - 15 = -21$ Then: $10 + (-21) = \rightarrow$ change addition into subtraction: $10 - 21 = -11$

MULTIPLYING AND DIVIDING INTEGERS

Use the following rules for multiplying and dividing integers:

☑ (negative) × (negative) = positive

☑ (negative) ÷ (negative) = positive

☑ (negative) × (positive) = negative

☑ (negative) ÷ (positive) = negative

☑ (positive) × (positive) = positive

☑ (positive) ÷ (negative) = negative

Examples:

Example 1. Solve. $2 \times (-3) =$

Solution: Use this rule: (positive) × (negative) = negative.
Then: $(2) \times (-3) = -6$

Example 2. Solve. $(-5) + (-27 \div 9) =$

Solution: First, divide -27 by 9, the numbers in brackets, use this rule:
(negative) ÷ (positive) = negative. Then: $-27 \div 9 = -3$
$(-5) + (-27 \div 9) = (-5) + (-3) = -5 - 3 = -8$

Example 3. Solve. $(15 - 17) \times (-8) =$

Solution: First, subtract the numbers in brackets,
$15 - 17 = -2 \rightarrow (-2) \times (-8) =$
Now use this rule: (negative) × (negative) = positive $\rightarrow (-2) \times (-8) = 16$

Example 4. Solve. $(16 - 10) \div (-2) =$

Solution: First, subtract the numbers in brackets,
$16 - 10 = 6 \rightarrow (6) \div (-2) =$
Now use this rule: (positive) ÷ (negative) = negative $\rightarrow (6) \div (-2) = -3$

ORDER OF OPERATIONS

☑ In Mathematics, "operations" are addition, subtraction, multiplication, division, exponentiation (written as b^n), and grouping;

☑ When there is more than one math operation in an expression, use PEMDAS: (to memorize this rule, remember the phrase "Please Excuse My Dear Aunt Sally".)

❖ Parentheses

❖ Exponents

❖ Multiplication and Division (from left to right)

❖ Addition and Subtraction (from left to right)

Examples:

Example 1. Calculate. $(3 + 5) \div (3^2 \div 9) =$

Solution: First, simplify inside parentheses:
$(8) \div (9 \div 9) = (8) \div (1)$, Then: $(8) \div (1) = 8$

Example 2. Solve. $(7 \times 8) - (12 - 4) =$

Solution: First, calculate within parentheses: $(7 \times 8) - (12 - 4) = (56) - (8)$, Then: $(56) - (8) = 48$

Example 3. Calculate. $-2[(8 \times 9) \div (2^2 \times 2)] =$

Solution: First, calculate within parentheses:
$-2[(72) \div (4 \times 2)] = -2[(72) \div (8)] = -2[9]$
multiply -2 and 9. Then: $-2[9] = -18$

Example 4. Solve. $(14 \div 7) + (-13 + 8) =$

Solution: First, calculate within parentheses:
$(14 \div 7) + (-13 + 8) = (2) + (-5)$ Then: $(2) - (5) = -3$

INTEGERS AND ABSOLUTE VALUE

Ø The absolute value of a number is its distance from zero, in either direction, on the number line. For example, the distance of 9 and -9 from zero on number line is 9.

Ø The absolute value of an integer is the numerical value without its sign. (negative or positive)

Ø The vertical bar is used for absolute value as in $|x|$.

Ø The absolute value of a number is never negative; because it only shows, "how far the number is from zero".

Examples:

Example 1. Calculate. $|12 - 4| \times 4 =$

Solution: First, solve $|12 - 4|$, $\rightarrow |12 - 4| = |8|$, the absolute value of 8 is 8, $|8| = 8$ Then: $8 \times 4 = 32$

Example 2. Solve. $\frac{|-16|}{4} \times |3 - 8| =$

Solution: First, find $|-16|$, $\rightarrow$ the absolute value of -16 is 16,
Then: $|-16| = 16$, $\frac{16}{4} \times |3 - 8| =$
Now, calculate $|3 - 8|$, $\rightarrow |3 - 8| = |-5|$, the absolute value of -5 is 5. $|-5| = 5$ then: $\frac{16}{4} \times 5 = 4 \times 5 = 20$

Example 3. Solve. $|9 - 3| \times \frac{|-3 \times 8|}{6} =$

Solution: First, calculate $|9 - 3|$, $\rightarrow |9 - 3| = |6|$, the absolute value of 6 is 6, $|6| = 6$. Then: $6 \times \frac{|-3 \times 8|}{6}$
Now calculate $|-3 \times 8|$, $\rightarrow |-3 \times 8| = |-24|$, the absolute value of -24 is 24, $|-24| = 24$ Then: $6 \times \frac{24}{6} = 6 \times 4 = 24$

CHAPTER 3: PRACTICES

✍ Find each sum or difference.

1) $13 - (-6) =$

2) $(-36) + 18 =$

3) $(-6) + (-22) =$

4) $54 + (-12) + 9 =$

5) $35 + (-24 + 4) =$

6) $(-17) + (-34 + 12) =$

7) $(-1) + (28 - 15) =$

8) $5 + (-9 + 12) =$

9) $(-10) + (-20) =$

10) $32 - (-5) =$

11) $(-9) + (24 - 3) =$

12) $8 - (-2 + 12) =$

13) $(-3) + (45 + 3) =$

14) $5 + (-30 + 6) =$

15) $(-6 + 1) + (-20) =$

16) $(-7) - (-20 + 2) =$

17) $(-6) - (2) =$

18) $(9 - 6) - (-3) =$

✍ Solve.

19) $4 \times (-8) =$

20) $(-27) \div (-9) =$

21) $(-2) \times (-9) \times 3 =$

22) $5 \times (-3) \times (-7) =$

23) $(-10 - 8) \div (-9) =$

24) $(-9 + 7) \times (-20) =$

25) $(-7) \times (-5) =$

26) $(-6) \times (-2 + 6) =$

27) $(-3) \times (-4) \times 3 =$

28) $(-8 - 2) \times (-1 + 4) =$

29) $(-9) \times (-20) =$

30) $6 \times (-2 + 9) =$

31) $(-5 - 6) \times (-2) =$

32) $(-4 - 2) \times (-3 - 7) =$

33) $(-9) \div (13 - 16) =$

34) $56 \times (-8) =$

35) $(-9 - 3) \div (-4) =$

36) $72 \div (-18 + 10) =$

✍ Evaluate each expression.

37) $2 + (6 \times 4) =$

38) $(7 \times 9) - 8 =$

39) $(-6) + (2 \times 9) =$

40) $(-2 - 4) + (3 \times 7) =$

41) $(28 \div 7) - (5 \times 3) =$

42) $(9 \times 3) + (6 \times 4) =$

43) $(36 \div 4) - (36 \div 6) =$

44) $(7 + 3) + (16 \div 2) =$

45) $(15 \times 3) - 16 =$

46) $8 - (7 \times 3) =$

47) $(9 + 15) \div (8 \div 4) =$

48) $2[(3 \times 6) + (16 \times 2)] =$

49) $(18 - 6) + (4 \times 2) =$

50) $2[(2 \times 3) - (8 \times 5)] =$

51) $(9 + 7) \div (16 \div 8) =$

52) $(3 + 9) \times (25 \times 2) =$

53) $3[(10 \times 9) \div (9 \times 5)] =$

54) $-6[(10 \times 9) \div (5 \times 6)] =$

✍ Find the answers.

55) $|-8| + |6 - 15| =$

56) $|-5 + 9| + |-3| =$

57) $|-6| + |2 - 10| =$

58) $|-8 + 3| - |4 - 8| =$

59) $|6 - 10| + |5 - 7| =$

60) $|-6| - |-9 - 19| + 5 =$

61) $|-9 + 2| - |3 - 5| + 6 =$

62) $4 + |3 - 7| + |2 - 6| =$

63) $\frac{|-64|}{8} \times \frac{|-48|}{6} =$

64) $\frac{|-36|}{6} \times \frac{|-56|}{8} =$

65) $\frac{|-72|}{9} \times \frac{|-45|}{5} =$

66) $|8 \times (-1)| \times \frac{|-24|}{3} =$

67) $|-2 \times 5| \times \frac{|-27|}{9} =$

68) $\frac{|-144|}{12} - |-6 \times 4| =$

69) $\frac{|-63|}{7} + |-9 \times 2| =$

70) $\frac{|-70|}{7} + |-8 \times 3| =$

71) $\frac{|-7 \times -3|}{7} \times \frac{|8 \times (-5)|}{8} =$

72) $\frac{|(-2) \times (-6)|}{4} \times \frac{|8 \times (-4)|}{2} =$

CHAPTER 3: ANSWERS

1) 19	25) 35	49) 20
2) −18	26) −24	50) −68
3) −28	27) 36	51) 8
4) 51	28) −30	52) 600
5) 15	29) 180	53) 6
6) −39	30) 42	54) −18
7) 12	31) 22	55) 17
8) 8	32) 80	56) 7
9) −30	33) 3	57) 14
10) 37	34) −448	58) 1
11) 12	35) 3	59) 6
12) −2	36) −9	60) −17
13) 45	37) 26	61) 11
14) −19	38) 55	62) 12
15) −25	39) 12	63) 64
16) 11	40) 15	64) 42
17) −8	41) −11	65) 72
18) 6	42) 51	66) 64
19) −32	43) 3	67) 30
20) 3	44) 18	68) −12
21) 54	45) 29	69) 27
22) 105	46) −13	70) 34
23) 2	47) 12	71) 15
24) 40	48) 100	72) 48

CHAPTER 4:

RATIOS AND PROPORTIONS

Math Topics that you'll learn in this chapter:

▶ Simplifying Ratios

▶ Proportional Ratios

▶ Similarity and Ratios

SIMPLIFYING RATIOS

☑ Ratios are used to make comparisons between two numbers.

☑ Ratios can be written as a fraction, using the word "to", or with a colon. Example: $\frac{3}{4}$ or "3 to 4" or 3:4

☑ You can calculate equivalent ratios by multiplying or dividing both sides of the ratio by the same number.

Examples:

Example 1. Simplify. $9:3 =$

Solution: Both numbers 9 and 3 are divisible by 3 , $\Rightarrow 9 \div 3 = 3$, $3 \div 3 = 1$, Then: $9:3 = 3:1$

Example 2. Simplify. $\frac{24}{44} =$

Solution: Both numbers 24 and 44 are divisible by 4, $\Rightarrow 24 \div 4 = 6$, $44 \div 4 = 11$, Then: $\frac{24}{44} = \frac{6}{11}$

Example 3. There are 36 students in a class and 16 are girls. Write the ratio of girls to boys.

Solution: Subtract 16 from 36 to find the number of boys in the class. $36 - 16 = 20$. There are 20 boys in the class. So, the ratio of girls to boys is $16:20$. Now, simplify this ratio. Both 20 and 16 are divisible by 4. Then: $20 \div 4 = 5$, and $16 \div 4 = 4$. In the simplest form, this ratio is $4:5$

Example 4. A recipe calls for butter and sugar in the ratio $3:4$. If you're using 9 cups of butter, how many cups of sugar should you use?

Solution: Since you use 9 cups of butter, or 3 times as much, you need to multiply the amount of sugar by 3. Then: $4 \times 3 = 12$. So, you need to use 12 cups of sugar. You can solve this using equivalent fractions: $\frac{3}{4} = \frac{9}{12}$

PROPORTIONAL RATIOS

☑ Two ratios are proportional if they represent the same relationship.

☑ A proportion means that two ratios are equal. It can be written in two ways:

$$\frac{a}{b} = \frac{c}{d} \qquad a : b = c : d$$

☑ The proportion $\frac{a}{b} = \frac{c}{d}$ can be written as: $a \times d = c \times b$

Examples:

Example 1. Solve this proportion for x. $\quad \frac{3}{7} = \frac{12}{x}$

Solution: Use cross multiplication: $\frac{3}{7} = \frac{12}{x} \Rightarrow 3 \times x = 7 \times 12 \Rightarrow 3x = 84$

Divide both sides by 3 to find x: $\quad x = \frac{84}{3} \Rightarrow x = 28$

Example 2. If a box contains red and blue balls in ratio of 3: 7 red to blue, how many red balls are there if 49 blue balls are in the box?

Solution: Write a proportion and solve. $\frac{3}{7} = \frac{x}{49}$

Use cross multiplication: $\quad 3 \times 49 = 7 \times x \Rightarrow 147 = 7x$

Divide to find x: $x = \frac{147}{7} \Rightarrow x = 21$. There are 21 red balls in the box.

Example 3. Solve this proportion for x. $\quad \frac{2}{9} = \frac{12}{x}$

Solution: Use cross multiplication: $\frac{2}{9} = \frac{12}{x} \Rightarrow 2 \times x = 9 \times 12 \Rightarrow 2x = 108$

Divide to find x: $x = \frac{108}{2} \Rightarrow x = 54$

Example 4. Solve this proportion for x. $\frac{6}{7} = \frac{18}{x}$

Solution: Use cross multiplication: $\frac{6}{7} = \frac{18}{x} \Rightarrow 6 \times x = 7 \times 18 \Rightarrow 6x = 126$

Divide to find x: $x = \frac{126}{6} \Rightarrow x = 21$

SIMILARITY AND RATIOS

☑ Two figures are similar if they have the same shape.

☑ Two or more figures are similar if the corresponding angles are equal, and the corresponding sides are in proportion.

Examples:

Example 1. The following triangles are similar. What is the value of the unknown side?

Solution: Find the corresponding sides and write a proportion.
$\frac{5}{10} = \frac{4}{x}$. Now, use the cross product to solve for x:
$\frac{5}{10} = \frac{4}{x} \rightarrow 5 \times x = 10 \times 4 \rightarrow 5x = 40$. Divide both sides by 5. Then: $5x = 40 \rightarrow \frac{5x}{5} = \frac{40}{5} \rightarrow x = 8$
The missing side is 8.

Example 2. Two rectangles are similar. The first is 6 feet wide and 20 feet long. The second is 15 feet wide. What is the length of the second rectangle?

Solution: Let's put x for the length of the second rectangle. Since two rectangles are similar, their corresponding sides are in proportion. Write a proportion and solve for the missing number.
$\frac{6}{15} = \frac{20}{x} \rightarrow 6x = 15 \times 20 \rightarrow 6x = 300 \rightarrow x = \frac{300}{6} = 50$
The length of the second rectangle is 50 feet.

CHAPTER 4: PRACTICES

✐ Reduce each ratio.

1) $3:21 = \underline{\quad}:\underline{\quad}$

2) $8:72 = \underline{\quad}:\underline{\quad}$

3) $21:49 = \underline{\quad}:\underline{\quad}$

4) $32:28 = \underline{\quad}:\underline{\quad}$

5) $35:45 = \underline{\quad}:\underline{\quad}$

6) $72:81 = \underline{\quad}:\underline{\quad}$

7) $36:54 = \underline{\quad}:\underline{\quad}$

8) $56:64 = \underline{\quad}:\underline{\quad}$

9) $12:36 = \underline{\quad}:\underline{\quad}$

10) $4:32 = \underline{\quad}:\underline{\quad}$

11) $16:48 = \underline{\quad}:\underline{\quad}$

12) $15:105 = \underline{\quad}:\underline{\quad}$

✐ Solve.

13) Bob has 18 red cards and 27 green cards. What is the ratio of Bob's red cards to his green cards? _____

14) In a party, 30 soft drinks are required for every 18 guests. If there are 240 guests, how many soft drinks are required? _____

15) Sara has 72 blue pens and 36 black pens. What is the ratio of Sara's black pens to her blue pens? _____

16) In Jack's class, 45 of the students are tall and 18 are short. In Michael's class 27 students are tall and 12 students are short. Which class has a higher ratio of tall to short students? _____

17) The price of 3 apples at the Quick Market is $1.44. The price of 5 of the same apples at Walmart is $2.45. Which place is the better buy? _____

18) The bakers at a Bakery can make 160 bagels in 4 hours. How many bagels can they bake in 14 hours? What is that rate per hour? _____

19) You can buy 5 cans of green beans at a supermarket for $3.40. How much does it cost to buy 35 cans of green beans? _____

✎ Solve each proportion.

20) $\frac{3}{4} = \frac{15}{x}$, $x =$

21) $\frac{9}{6} = \frac{x}{4}$, $x =$ _____

22) $\frac{3}{15} = \frac{2}{x}$, $x =$ _____

23) $\frac{5}{15} = \frac{3}{x}$, $x =$ _____

24) $\frac{24}{3} = \frac{x}{2}$, $x =$ _____

25) $\frac{8}{12} = \frac{10}{x}$, $x =$ ____

26) $\frac{3}{x} = \frac{2}{14}$, $x =$ ___

27) $\frac{10}{x} = \frac{3}{6}$, $x =$ ____

28) $\frac{15}{6} = \frac{x}{4}$, $x =$ ____

29) $\frac{x}{12} = \frac{5}{10}$, $x =$ ___

30) $\frac{18}{6} = \frac{3}{x}$, $x =$ ___

31) $\frac{3}{4} = \frac{24}{x}$, $x =$ _____

32) $\frac{8}{4} = \frac{x}{2}$, $x =$ _____

33) $\frac{12}{3} = \frac{x}{4}$, $x =$ _____

34) $\frac{24}{8} = \frac{x}{2}$, $x =$ _____

35) $\frac{5}{3} = \frac{x}{6}$, $x =$ _____

36) $\frac{10}{8} = \frac{x}{4}$, $x =$ _____

37) $\frac{x}{6} = \frac{6}{4}$, $x =$ _____

38) $\frac{x}{4} = \frac{7}{2}$, $x =$ _____

39) $\frac{9}{x} = \frac{3}{4}$, $x =$ _____

40) $\frac{10}{x} = \frac{1}{5}$, $x =$ _____

41) $\frac{9}{2} = \frac{x}{8}$, $x =$ _____

✎ Solve each problem.

42) Two rectangles are similar. The first is 6 *feet* wide and 24 *feet* long. The second is 10 *feet* wide. What is the length of the second rectangle? _____

43) Two rectangles are similar. One is 4.8 *meters* by 6 *meters*. The longer side of the second rectangle is 27 *meters*. What is the other side of the second rectangle? _____

CHAPTER 4: ANSWERS

1) $1:7$
2) $1:9$
3) $3:7$
4) $8:7$
5) $7:9$
6) $8:9$
7) $2:3$
8) $7:8$
9) $1:3$
10) $1:8$
11) $1:3$
12) $1:7$
13) $2:3$
14) 144
15) $1:2$
16) $jack's\ class = \frac{45}{18} = \frac{5}{2}$
$Michael's\ class = \frac{27}{12} = \frac{9}{4}$
Jack's class has a higher ratio of tall to short student
17) Quick Market
18) 560
19) $\$23.80$
20) 20

21) 6
22) 10
23) 9
24) 16
25) 15
26) 21
27) 20
28) 10
29) 6
30) 1
31) 32
32) 16
33) 16
34) 6
35) 1
36) 5
37) 9
38) 14
39) 12
40) 50
41) 36
42) 40
43) $21.6\ meters$

CHAPTER 5:

PERCENTAGE

Math Topics that you'll learn in this chapter:

► Percentage Calculations

► Percent Problems

► Percent of Increase and Decrease

► Discount, Tax and Tip

► Simple Interest

PERCENT PROBLEMS

☑ Percent is a ratio of a number and 100. It always has the same denominator, 100. The percent symbol is "%".

☑ Percent means "per 100". So, 20% is 20/100.

☑ In each percent problem, we are looking for the base, or part or the percent.

☑ Use these equations to find each missing section in a percent problem:

    ❖ Base = Part ÷ Percent

    ❖ Part = Percent × Base

    ❖ Percent = Part ÷ Base

Examples:

Example 1. What is 25% of 60?

Solution: In this problem, we have percent (25%) and base (60) and we are looking for the "part". Use this formula: $part = percent \times base$. Then: $part = 25\% \times 60 = \frac{25}{100} \times 60 = 0.25 \times 60 = 15$. The answer: 25% of 60 is 15.

Example 2. 20 is what percent of 400?

Solution: In this problem, we are looking for the percent. Use this equation: $Percent = Part \div Base \rightarrow Percent = 20 \div 400 = 0.05 = 5\%$. Then: 20 is 5 percent of 400.

PERCENT OF INCREASE AND DECREASE

☑ Percent of change (increase or decrease) is a mathematical concept that represents the degree of change over time.

☑ To find the percentage of increase or decrease:

    1. New Number – Original Number

    2. The result ÷ Original Number × 100

☑ Or use this formula: Percent of change $= \frac{new\ number - original\ number}{original\ number} \times 100$

☑ Note: If your answer is a negative number, then this is a percentage decrease. If it is positive, then this is a percentage increase.

Examples:

Example 1. The price of a shirt increases from $20 to $30. What is the percentage increase?

Solution: First, find the difference: $30 - 20 = 10$

Then: $10 \div 20 \times 100 = \frac{10}{20} \times 100 = 50$. The percentage increase is 50. It means that the price of the shirt increased by 50%.

Example 2. The price of a table increased from $25 to $40. What is the percent of increase?

Solution: Use percentage formula:

$$Percent\ of\ change = \frac{new\ number - original\ number}{original\ number} \times 100 =$$

$\frac{40-25}{25} \times 100 = \frac{15}{25} \times 100 = 0.6 \times 100 = 60$. The percentage increase is 60. It means that the price of the table increased by 60%.

DISCOUNT, TAX AND TIP

☑ To find the discount: Multiply the regular price by the rate of discount

☑ To find the selling price: Original price − discount

☑ To find tax: Multiply the tax rate to the taxable amount (income, property value, etc.)

☑ To find the tip, multiply the rate to the selling price.

Examples:

Example 1. With an 10% discount, Ella saved $45 on a dress. What was the original price of the dress?

Solution: let x be the original price of the dress. Then: $10 \% \ of \ x = 45$. Write an equation and solve for x: $0.10 \times x = 45 \rightarrow x = \frac{45}{0.10} = 450$. The original price of the dress was $450.

Example 2. Sophia purchased a new computer for a price of $950 at the Apple Store. What is the total amount her credit card is charged if the sales tax is 7%?

Solution: The taxable amount is $950, and the tax rate is 7%. Then:
$Tax = 0.07 \times 950 = 66.50$
$Final \ price = Selling \ price + Tax \rightarrow final \ price = \$950 + \$66.50 = \$1,016.50$

Example 3. Nicole and her friends went out to eat at a restaurant. If their bill was $80.00 and they gave their server a 15% tip, how much did they pay altogether?

Solution: First, find the tip. To find the tip, multiply the rate to the bill amount. $Tip = 80 \times 0.15 = 12$. The final price is: $\$80 + \$12 = \$92$

SIMPLE INTEREST

Ø Simple Interest: The charge for borrowing money or the return for lending it.

Ø Simple interest is calculated on the initial amount (principal).

Ø To solve a simple interest problem, use this formula:

Interest = principal x rate x time $(I = p \times r \times t = prt)$

Examples:

Example 1. Find simple interest for $300 investment at 6% for 5 years.

Solution: Use Interest formula:
$I = prt$ ($P = \$300$, r = 6% = $\frac{6}{100}$ = 0.06 and $t = 5$)
Then: $I = 300 \times 0.06 \times 5 = \$90$

Example 2. Find simple interest for $1,600 at 5% for 2 years.

Solution: Use Interest formula:
$I = prt$ ($P = \$1,600$, r = 5% = $\frac{5}{100}$ = 0.05 and $t = 2$)
Then: $I = 1,600 \times 0.05 \times 2 = \$160$

Example 3. Andy received a student loan to pay for his educational expenses this year. What is the interest on the loan if he borrowed $6,500 at 8% for 6 years?

Solution: Use Interest formula:$I = prt$. $P = \$6,500$, r = 8% = 0.08 and $t = 6$
Then: $I = 6,500 \times 0.08 \times 8 = \$3,120$

Example 4. Bob is starting his own small business. He borrowed $10,000 from the bank at a 6% rate for 6 months. Find the interest Bob will pay on this loan.

Solution: Use Interest formula:
$I = prt$. $P = \$10,000$, r = 6% = 0.06 and $t = 0.5$ (6 months is half year).
Then: $I = 10,000 \times 0.06 \times 0.5 = \$300$

CHAPTER 5: PRACTICES

🖎 Solve each problem.

1) 10 is what percent of 80? ____%

2) 12 is what percent of 60? ____%

3) 20 is what percent of 80? ____%

4) 18 is what percent of 72? ____%

5) 16 is what percent of 50? ____%

6) 35 is what percent of 140? ____%

7) 12 is what percent of 240? ____%

8) 80 is what percent of 400? ____%

9) 60 is what percent of 300? ____%

10) 100 is what percent of 250? ____%

11) 25 is what percent of 400? ____%

12) 60 is what percent of 480? ____%

🖎 Solve each problem.

13) Bob got a raise, and his hourly wage increased from $16 to $20. What is the percent increase? _____ %

14) The price of a pair of shoes increases from $30 to $36. What is the percent increase? ___ %

15) At a coffeeshop, the price of a cup of coffee increased from $1.30 to $1.56. What is the percent increase in the cost of the coffee? _____ %

16) A $40 shirt now selling for $28 is discounted by what percent? _____ %

17) Joe scored 20 out of 25 marks in Algebra, 30 out of 40 marks in science and 68 out of 80 marks in mathematics. In which subject his percentage of marks is best? _____

18) Emma purchased a computer for $408. The computer is regularly priced at $480. What was the percent discount Emma received on the computer? _____

19) A chemical solution contains 12% alcohol. If there is 42 ml of alcohol, what is the volume of the solution? _____

✎ Find the selling price of each item.

20) Original price of a computer: $700

 Tax: 9%, Selling price: $_____

21) Original price of a laptop: $460

 Tax: 20%, Selling price: $_____

22) Nicolas hired a moving company. The company charged $600 for its services, and Nicolas gives the movers a 12% tip. How much does Nicolas tip the movers? $_____

23) Mason has lunch at a restaurant and the cost of his meal is $50. Mason wants to leave a 25% tip. What is Mason's total bill, including tip? $_____

✎ Determine the simple interest for the following loans.

24) $480 *at* 6% *for* 5 *years.* $___

25) $500 *at* 5% *for* 3 *years.* $___

26) $360 *at* 3.5% *for* 2 *years.* $___

27) $600 at 4% for 4 years. $___

✎ Solve.

28) A new car, valued at $25,000, depreciates at 7% per year. What is the value of the car one year after purchase? $_____

29) Sara puts $6,000 into an investment yielding 4% annual simple interest; she left the money in for five years. How much interest does Sara get at the end of those five years? $_____

CHAPTER 5: ANSWERS

1) 12.5%

2) 20%

3) 25%

4) 25%

5) 32%

6) 25%

7) 5%

8) 20%

9) 20%

10) 40%

11) 6.25%

12) 12.5%

13) 25%

14) 20%

15) 20%

16) 30%

17) Mathematics

18) 15%

19) 350

20) $763

21) $552

22) $72

23) $62.50

24) $144

25) $75

26) $25.20

27) $96

28) $23,250

29) $1200

CHAPTER 6:

EXPRESSIONS AND VARIABLES

Math Topics that you'll learn in this chapter:

▶ Simplifying Variable Expressions

▶ Simplifying Polynomial Expressions

▶ The Distributive Property

▶ Evaluating One Variable

▶ Evaluating Two Variables

SIMPLIFYING VARIABLE EXPRESSIONS

☑ In algebra, a variable is a letter used to stand for a number. The most common letters are $x, y, z, a, b, c, m, and\ n$.

☑ An algebraic expression is an expression that contains integers, variables, and math operations such as addition, subtraction, multiplication, division, etc.

☑ In an expression, we can combine "like" terms. (values with same variable and same power)

Examples:

Example 1. Simplify. $(2x + 3x + 4) =$

Solution: In this expression, there are three terms: $2x, 3x$, and 4. Two terms are "like terms": $2x$ and $3x$. Combine like terms. $2x + 3x = 5x$. Then: $(2x + 3x + 4) = 5x + 4$ (***remember you cannot combine variables and numbers.***)

Example 2. Simplify. $12 - 3x^2 + 5x + 4x^2 =$

Solution: Combine "like" terms: $-3x^2 + 4x^2 = x^2$.
Then: $12 - 3x^2 + 5x + 4x^2 = 12 + x^2 + 5x$. Write in standard form (biggest powers first): $12 + x^2 + 5x = x^2 + 5x + 12$

Example 3. Simplify. $(10x^2 + 2x^2 + 3x) =$

Solution: Combine like terms. Then: $(10x^2 + 2x^2 + 3x) = 12x^2 + 3x$

Example 4. Simplify. $15x - 3x^2 + 9x + 5x^2 =$

Solution: Combine "like" terms: $15x + 9x = 24x$, and $-3x^2 + 5x^2 = 2x^2$
Then: $15x - 3x^2 + 9x + 5x^2 = 24x + 2x^2$. Write in standard form (biggest powers first): $24x + 2x^2 = 2x^2 + 24x$

SIMPLIFYING POLYNOMIAL EXPRESSIONS

☑ In mathematics, a polynomial is an expression consisting of variables and coefficients that involves only the operations of addition, subtraction, multiplication, and non–negative integer exponents of variables. $P(x) = a_n x^n + a_{n-1} x^{n-1} + \dots + a_2 x^2 + a_1 x + a_0$

☑ Polynomials must always be simplified as much as possible. It means you must add together any like terms. (values with same variable and same power)

Examples:

Example 1. Simplify this Polynomial Expressions. $x^2 - 5x^3 + 2x^4 - 4x^3$

Solution: Combine "like" terms: $-5x^3 - 4x^3 = -9x^3$
Then: $x^2 - 5x^3 + 2x^4 - 4x^3 = x^2 - 9x^3 + 2x^4$
Now, write the expression in standard form: $2x^4 - 9x^3 + x^2$

Example 2. Simplify this expression. $(2x^2 - x^3) - (x^3 - 4x^2) =$

Solution: First, use distributive property: → multiply (−) into $(x^3 - 4x^2)$
$(2x^2 - x^3) - (x^3 - 4x^2) = 2x^2 - x^3 - x^3 + 4x^2$
Then combine "like" terms: $2x^2 - x^3 - x^3 + 4x^2 = 6x^2 - 2x^3$
And write in standard form: $6x^2 - 2x^3 = -2x^3 + 6x^2$

Example 3. Simplify. $4x^4 - 5x^3 + 15x^4 - 12x^3 =$

Solution: Combine "like" terms:
$-5x^3 - 12x^3 = -17x^3$ and $4x^4 + 15x^4 = 19x^4$
Then: $4x^4 - 5x^3 + 15x^4 - 12x^3 = 19x^4 - 17x^3$

THE DISTRIBUTIVE PROPERTY

☑ The distributive property (or the distributive property of multiplication over addition and subtraction) simplifies and solves expressions in the form of: $a(b + c)$ or $a(b - c)$

☑ The distributive property is multiplying a term outside the parentheses by the terms inside.

☑ Distributive Property rule: $a(b + c) = ab + ac$

Examples:

Example 1. Simply using the distributive property. $(-4)(x - 5)$

Solution: Use Distributive Property rule: $a(b + c) = ab + ac$
$(-4)(x - 5) = (-4 \times x) + (-4) \times (-5) = -4x + 20$

Example 2. Simply. $(3)(2x - 4)$

Solution: Use Distributive Property rule: $a(b + c) = ab + ac$
$(3)(2x - 4) = (3 \times 2x) + (3) \times (-4) = 6x - 12$

Example 3. Simply. $(-3)(3x - 5) + 4x$

Solution: First, simplify $(-3)(3x - 5)$ using the distributive property.
Then: $(-3)(3x - 5) = -9x + 15$
Now combine like terms: $(-3)(3x - 5) + 4x = -9x + 15 + 4x$
In this expression, $-9x$ and $4x$ are "like terms" and we can combine them.
$-9x + 4x = -5x$. Then: $-9x + 15 + 4x = -5x + 15$

EVALUATING ONE VARIABLE

☑ To evaluate one variable expression, find the variable and substitute a number for that variable.

☑ Perform the arithmetic operations.

Examples:

Example 1. Calculate this expression for x = 3. $15 - 3x$

Solution: First, substitute 3 for x
Then: $15 - 3x = 15 - 3(3)$
Now, use order of operation to find the answer: $15 - 3(3) = 15 - 9 = 6$

Example 2. Evaluate this expression for x = 1. $5x - 12$

Solution: First, substitute 1 for x,
Then: $5x - 12 = 5(1) - 12$
Now, use order of operation to find the answer: $5(1) - 12 = 5 - 12 = -7$

Example 3. Find the value of this expression when x = 5. $25 - 4x$

Solution: First, substitute 5 for x,
Then: $25 - 4x = 25 - 4(5) = 25 - 20 = 5$

Example 4. Solve this expression for $x = -2$. $12 + 3x$

Solution: Substitute −2 for x,
Then: $12 + 3x = 12 + 3(-2) = 12 - 6 = 6$

EVALUATING TWO VARIABLES

☑ To evaluate an algebraic expression, substitute a number for each variable.

☑ Perform the arithmetic operations to find the value of the expression.

Examples:

Example 1. Calculate this expression for a = 3 and $b = -2$. $3a - 6b$

Solution: First, substitute 3 for a, and -2 for b ,
Then: $3a - 6b = 3(3) - 6(-2)$
Now, use order of operation to find the answer: $3(3) - 6(-2) = 9 + 12 = 21$

Example 2. Evaluate this expression for x = 3 and $y = 1$. $3x + 5y$

Solution: Substitute 3 for x, and 1 for y ,
Then: $3x + 5y = 3(3) + 5(1) = 9 + 5 = 14$

Example 3. Find the value of this expression $5(3a - 2b)$ when $a = 1$ and $b = 2$.

Solution: Substitute 1 for a, and 2 for b ,
Then: $5(3a - 2b) = 15a - 10b = 15(1) - 10(2) = 15 - 20 = -5$

Example 4. Solve this expression. $4x - 3y$, $x = 3$, $y = 5$

Solution: Substitute 3 for x, and 5 for y and simplify.
Then: $4x - 3y = 4(3) - 3(5) = 12 - 15 = -3$

CHAPTER 6: PRACTICES

✎ Simplify each expression.

1) $(9x - 5x - 7 + 4) =$

2) $(-12x - 7x + 6 - 3) =$

3) $(24x - 10x - 3) =$

4) $(-10x + 23x - 6) =$

5) $(32x + 8 - 20x - 4) =$

6) $3 + 6x^2 - 6 =$

7) $3x + 6x^4 - 6x =$

8) $-1 - 2x^2 - 8 =$

9) $67 + 6x - 1 - 9 =$

10) $3x^2 + 9x - 11x - 2 =$

11) $-3x^2 - 5x - 7x + 6 - 7 =$

12) $9x - 2x^2 + 8x =$

13) $12x^2 + 6x - 3x^2 + 12 =$

14) $10x^2 - 8x - 5x^2 + 4 =$

✎ Simplify each polynomial.

15) $8x^2 + 2x^3 - 4x^2 + 10x =$

16) $6x^4 + 3x^5 - 9x^4 + 7x^2 =$

17) $10x^3 + 12x - 3x^2 - 7x^3 =$

18) $(6x^3 - 2x^2) + (4x^2 - 14x) =$

19) $(13x^4 + 5x^3) + (2x^3 - 6x^4) =$

20) $(14x^5 - 9x^3) - (3x^3 + x^2) =$

21) $(10x^4 + 6x^3) - (x^3 - 65) =$

22) $(26x^4 + 5x^3) - (15x^3 - 3x^4) =$

23) $(10x^2 + 8x^3) + (25x^2 + 4x^3) =$

24) $(8x^4 - 3x^3) + (4x^3 - 7x^4) =$

✎ Use the distributive property to simply each expression.

25) $3(6 + 9x) =$ _____

26) $6(4 - 3x) =$ _____

27) $(-8)(3 - 4x) =$ _____

28) $(2 - 5x)(-6) =$ _____

29) $3(7 - 2x) =$

30) $(-x + 1)(-9) =$ _____

31) $(-3)(9x - 5) =$ _____

32) $(2x + 10)6 =$ _____

33) $(-1)(1 - 3x) =$ _____

34) $(6x - 1)(-9) =$ _____

✎ Evaluate each expression using the value given.

35) $x = -5,\quad 14 - x =$ ____

36) $x = -7,\quad x + 10 =$ ____

37) $x = 4,\quad 6x - 8 =$ ____

38) $x = 3,\quad 9 - 3x =$ ____

39) $x = -8,\quad 6x - 9 =$ ____

40) $x = 7,\quad 18 - 3x =$ ____

41) $x = -1,\quad 14x - 3 =$ ____

42) $x = 5,\quad 10 - x =$ ____

43) $x = 2,\quad 28 - 5x =$ ____

44) $x = -9,\quad 100 - 6x =$ ____

45) $x = 10,\quad 50 - 8x =$ ____

46) $x = 3,\quad 61x - 3 =$ ____

47) $x = 3,\quad 25x - 2 =$ ____

48) $x = -1,\quad 13 - 4x =$ ____

✎ Evaluate each expression using the values given.

49) $x = 2, y = -1,\quad 3x - 6y =$ _____

50) $a = 3, b = 6,\quad 7a + 2b =$ _____

51) $x = 3, y = 2,\quad 5x - 23y + 9 =$ _____

52) $a = 7, b = 5,\quad -9a + 3b + 8 =$ _____

53) $x = 3, y = 6,\quad 3x + 15 + 6y =$ _____

CHAPTER 6: ANSWERS

1) $4x - 3$

2) $-19x + 3$

3) $14x - 3$

4) $13x - 6$

5) $12x - 4$

6) $6x^2 - 3$

7) $6x^4 - 3x$

8) $-2x^2 - 9$

9) $6x + 57$

10) $10x^2 - 2x - 2$

11) $-3x^2 - 12x - 1$

12) $-2x^2 + 17x$

13) $9x^2 + 6x + 12$

14) $5x^2 - 8x + 4$

15) $2x^3 + 4x^2 + 10x$

16) $3x^5 - 3x^4 + 7x$

17) $3x^3 - 3x^2 + 12x$

18) $6x^3 + 2x^2 - 14x$

19) $7x^4 + 7x^3$

20) $14x^5 - 12x^3 - x^2$

21) $10x^4 + 5x^3 + 65$

22) $29x^4 - 10x^3$

23) $12x^3 + 35x^2$

24) $x^4 + x^3$

25) $27x + 18$

26) $-18x + 24$

27) $32x - 24$

28) $30x - 12$

29) $-6x + 21$

30) $9x - 9$

31) $-27x + 15$

32) $12x + 60$

33) $3x - 1$

34) $-54x + 9$

35) 19

36) 3

37) 16

38) 0

39) -57

40) -3

41) -17

42) 5

43) 18

44) 154

45) -30

46) 180

47) 73

48) 17

49) 12

50) 33

51) -22

52) -40

53) 60

CHAPTER 7:

EQUATIONS AND INEQUALITIES

Math Topics that you'll learn in this chapter:

► One-Step Equations

► Multi-Step Equations

► System of Equations

► Graphing Single–Variable Inequalities

► One-Step Inequalities

► Multi-Step Inequalities

ONE–STEP EQUATIONS

☑ The values of two expressions on both sides of an equation are equal. Example: $ax = b$. In this equation, ax is equal to b.

☑ Solving an equation means finding the value of the variable.

☑ You only need to perform one Math operation to solve the one-step equations.

☑ To solve a one-step equation, find the inverse (opposite) operation is being performed.

☑ The inverse operations are:

    ❖ Addition and subtraction

    ❖ Multiplication and division

Examples:

Example 1. Solve this equation for x. $3x = 18, x = ?$

Solution: Here, the operation is multiplication (variable x is multiplied by 3) and its inverse operation is division. To solve this equation, divide both sides of equation by 3: $3x = 18 \rightarrow \frac{3x}{3} = \frac{18}{3} \rightarrow x = 6$

Example 2. Solve this equation. $x + 15 = 0$, $x = ?$

Solution: In this equation 15 is added to the variable x. The inverse operation of addition is subtraction. To solve this equation, subtract 15 from both sides of the equation: $x + 15 - 15 = 0 - 15$. Then: $\rightarrow x = -15$

Example 3. Solve this equation for x. $x + 23 = 0$

Solution: Here, the operation is subtraction and its inverse operation is addition. To solve this equation, add 23 to both sides of the equation: $x + 23 - 23 = 0 - 23 \rightarrow x = -23$

MULTI–STEP EQUATIONS

☒ To solve a multi-step equation, combine "like" terms on one side.

☒ Bring variables to one side by adding or subtracting.

☒ Simplify using the inverse of addition or subtraction.

☒ Simplify further by using the inverse of multiplication or division.

☒ Check your solution by plugging the value of the variable into the original equation.

Examples:

Example 1. Solve this equation for x. $3x + 6 = 16 - 2x$

Solution: First, bring variables to one side by adding $2x$ to both sides. Then: $3x + 6 = 16 - 2x \rightarrow 3x + 6 + 2x = 16 - 2x + 2x$.

Simplify: $5x + 6 = 16$ Now, subtract 6 from both sides of the equation:

$5x + 6 - 6 = 16 - 6 \rightarrow 5x = 10 \rightarrow$ Divide both sides by 5:

$5x = 10 \rightarrow \dfrac{5x}{5} = \dfrac{10}{5} \rightarrow x = 2$

Let's check this solution by substituting the value of 2 for x in the original equation:

$x = 2 \rightarrow 3x + 6 = 16 - 2x \rightarrow 3(2) + 6 = 16 - 2(2) \rightarrow 6 + 6 = 16 - 4 \rightarrow 12 = 12$

The answer $x = 2$ is correct.

Example 2. Solve this equation for x. $-4x + 4 = 16$

Solution: Subtract 4 from both sides of the equation.

$-4x + 4 - 4 = 16 - 4 \rightarrow -4x = 12$

Divide both sides by -4, then: $-4x = 12 \rightarrow \dfrac{-4x}{-4} = \dfrac{12}{-4} \rightarrow x = -3$

Now, check the solution:

$x = -3 \rightarrow -4x + 4 = 16 \rightarrow -4(-3) + 4 = 16 \rightarrow 16 = 16$

The answer $x = -2$ is correct.

SYSTEM OF EQUATIONS

☑ A system of equations contains two equations and two variables. For example, consider the system of equations: $x - y = 1, x + y = 5$

☑ The easiest way to solve a system of equations is using the elimination method. The elimination method uses the addition property of equality. You can add the same value to each side of an equation.

☑ For the first equation above, you can add $x + y$ to the left side and 5 to the right side of the first equation: $x - y + (x + y) = 1 + 5$. Now, if you simplify, you get: $x - y + (x + y) = 1 + 5 \rightarrow 2x = 6 \rightarrow x = 3$. Now, substitute 3 for the x in the first equation: $3 - y = 1$. By solving this equation, $y = 2$

Example:

What is the value of x + y in this system of equations?

$$\begin{cases} x + 2y = 6 \\ 2x - y = -8 \end{cases}$$

Solution: Solving a System of Equations by Elimination:
Multiply the first equation by (-2), then add it to the second equation.

$$\begin{array}{l} -2(x + 2y = 6) \\ \underline{2x - y = -8} \end{array} \Rightarrow \begin{array}{l} -2x - 4y = -12 \\ 2x - y = -8 \end{array} \Rightarrow -5y = -20 \Rightarrow y = 4$$

Plug in the value of y into one of the equations and solve for x.
$x + 2(4) = 6 \Rightarrow x + 8 = 6 \Rightarrow x = 6 - 8 \Rightarrow x = -2$
Thus, $x + y = -2 + 4 = 2$

GRAPHING SINGLE–VARIABLE INEQUALITIES

- ☑ An inequality compares two expressions using an inequality sign.

- ☑ Inequality signs are: "less than" <, "greater than" >, "less than or equal to" ≤, and "greater than or equal to" ≥.

- ☑ To graph a single–variable inequality, find the value of the inequality on the number line.

- ☑ For less than (<) or greater than (>) draw an open circle on the value of the variable. If there is an equal sign too, then use a filled circle.

- ☑ Draw an arrow to the right for greater or to the left for less than.

Examples:

Example 1. Draw a graph for this inequality. $x > 3$

Solution: Since the variable is greater than 3, then we need to find 3 in the number line and draw an open circle on it. Then, draw an arrow to the right.

Example 2. Graph this inequality. $x \leq -4$.

Solution: Since the variable is less than or equal to −4, then we need to find −4 in the number line and draw a filled circle on it. Then, draw an arrow to the left.

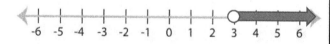

ONE–STEP INEQUALITIES

- ☑ An inequality compares two expressions using an inequality sign.
- ☑ Inequality signs are: "less than" <, "greater than" >, "less than or equal to" ≤, and "greater than or equal to" ≥.
- ☑ You only need to perform one Math operation to solve the one-step inequalities.
- ☑ To solve one-step inequalities, find the inverse (opposite) operation is being performed.
- ☑ For dividing or multiplying both sides by negative numbers, flip the direction of the inequality sign.

Examples:

Example 1. Solve this inequality for x. x + 3 ≥ 4

Solution: The inverse (opposite) operation of addition is subtraction. In this inequality, 3 is added to x. To isolate x we need to subtract 3 from both sides of the inequality.

Then: $x + 3 \geq 4 \rightarrow x + 3 - 3 \geq 4 - 3 \rightarrow x \geq 1$. The solution is: $x \geq 1$

Example 2. Solve the inequality. $x - 5 > -4$.

Solution: 5 is subtracted from x. Add 5 to both sides.

$x - 5 > -4 \rightarrow x - 5 + 5 > -4 + 5 \rightarrow x > 1$

Example 3. Solve. $2x \leq -4$.

Solution: 2 is multiplied to x. Divide both sides by 2.

Then: $2x \leq -4 \rightarrow \frac{2x}{2} \leq \frac{-4}{2} \rightarrow x \leq -2$

Example 4. Solve. $-6x \leq 12$.

Solution: -6 is multiplied to x. Divide both sides by -6. Remember when dividing or multiplying both sides of an inequality by negative numbers, flip the direction of the inequality sign.

Then: $-6x \leq 12 \rightarrow \frac{-6x}{-6} \geq \frac{12}{-6} \rightarrow x \geq -2$

MULTI–STEP INEQUALITIES

☑ To solve a multi-step inequality, combine "like" terms on one side.

☑ Bring variables to one side by adding or subtracting.

☑ Isolate the variable.

☑ Simplify using the inverse of addition or subtraction.

☑ Simplify further by using the inverse of multiplication or division.

☑ For dividing or multiplying both sides by negative numbers, flip the direction of the inequality sign.

Examples:

Example 1. Solve this inequality. $2x - 3 \leq 5$

Solution: In this inequality, 3 is subtracted from $2x$. The inverse of subtraction is addition. Add 3 to both sides of the inequality:
$2x - 3 + 3 \leq 5 + 3 \rightarrow 2x \leq 8$
Now, divide both sides by 2. Then: $2x \leq 8 \rightarrow \frac{2x}{2} \leq \frac{8}{2} \rightarrow x \leq 4$
The solution of this inequality is $x \leq 4$.

Example 2. Solve this inequality. $3x + 9 < 12$

Solution: First, subtract 9 from both sides: $3x + 9 - 9 < 12 - 9$
Then simplify: $3x + 9 - 9 < 12 - 9 \rightarrow 3x < 3$
Now divide both sides by 3: $\frac{3x}{3} < \frac{3}{3} \rightarrow x < 1$

Example 3. Solve this inequality. $-2x + 4 \geq 6$

Solution: First, subtract 4 from both sides:
$-2x + 4 - 4 \geq 6 - 4 \rightarrow -2x \geq 2$
Divide both sides by -2. Remember that you need to flip the direction of inequality sign. $-2x \geq 2 \rightarrow \frac{-2x}{-2} \leq \frac{2}{-2} \rightarrow x \leq -1$

CHAPTER 7: PRACTICES

✍ Solve each equation. (One–Step Equations)

1) $x + 8 = 4, x =$ _____

2) $3 = 12 - x, x =$ _____

3) $-4 = 9 + x, x =$ _____

4) $x - 6 = -9, x =$ _____

5) $18 = x + 8, x =$ _____

6) $15 - x = -4, x =$ _____

7) $25 - x = 8, x =$ _____

8) $6 + x = 27, x =$ _____

9) $10 - x = -8, x =$ _____

10) $36 - x = -5, x =$ _____

✍ Solve each equation. (Multi–Step Equations)

11) $6(x + 8) = 24, \ x =$ ____

12) $-9(9 - x) = 18, \ x =$ ____

13) $7 = -7(x + 3), \ x =$ ____

14) $-16 = 2(10 - 6x), \ x =$ ____

15) $6(x + 1) = -24, \ x =$ ____

16) $-3(7 + 9x) = 33, \ x =$ ____

17) $-7(5 - x) = 14, \ x =$ ____

18) $-1(3 - x) = 10, \ x =$ ____

✍ Solve each system of equations.

19) $\begin{cases} -2x + 2y = -4 \\ 4x - 9y = 28 \end{cases}$ $\quad \begin{aligned} x = \\ y = \end{aligned}$

20) $\begin{cases} x + 8y = -5 \\ 2x + 6y = 0 \end{cases}$ $\quad \begin{aligned} x = \\ y = \end{aligned}$

21) $\begin{cases} 4x - 3y = -2 \\ x - y = 3 \end{cases}$ $\quad \begin{aligned} x = \\ y = \end{aligned}$

22) $\begin{cases} 2x + 9y = 17 \\ -3x + 8y = 39 \end{cases}$ $\quad \begin{aligned} x = \\ y = \end{aligned}$

✎ **Draw a graph for each inequality.**

23) $x \leq -3$

24) $x > -5$

✎ **Solve each inequality and graph it.**

25) $x - 2 \geq -2$

26) $2x - 3 < 9$

✎ **Solve each inequality.**

27) $4x + 12 > -8$

28) $3x + 14 > 5$

29) $-16 + 3x \leq 20$

30) $-18 + 6x \leq -24$

31) $8 + 2x \leq 16$

32) $5(x + 2) \geq 6$

33) $2(3 + x) \geq 10$

34) $6x - 10 < 14$

35) $12x + 8 < 32$

36) $8(4 + x) \geq 16$

37) $2(x - 5) \geq 18$

38) $x + 10 < 3$

39) $2(x - 4) \geq 20$

40) $-8 + 9x > 28$

41) $-4 + 8x > 60$

42) $-2 + 7x > 40$

CHAPTER 7: ANSWERS

1) -4

2) 9

3) -13

4) -3

5) 10

6) 19

7) 17

8) 21

9) 18

10) 41

11) -4

12) 11

13) -4

14) 3

15) -5

16) -2

17) 7

18) 13

19) $x = -2, y = -4$

20) $x = 3, y = -1$

21) $x = -11, y = -14$

22) $x = -5, y = 3$

23) $\quad x \le -3$

24) $\quad x > -5$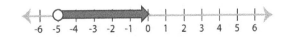

25) $\quad x \ge 0$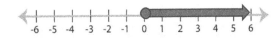

26) $\quad x < 6$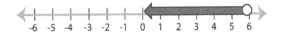

27) $x > -5$

28) $x > -3$

29) $x \le 12$

30) $x \le -1$

31) $x \le 4$

32) $x \ge -\frac{4}{5}$

33) $x \ge 2$

34) $x < 4$

35) $x < 2$

36) $x \ge -2$

37) $x \ge 14$

38) $x < -7$

39) $x \ge 14$

40) $x > 4$

41) $x > 8$

42) $x > 6$

CHAPTER 8:

LINES AND SLOPE

Math Topics that you'll learn in this chapter:

- ▶ Finding Slope
- ▶ Graphing Lines Using Slope–Intercept Form
- ▶ Writing Linear Equations
- ▶ Graphing Linear Inequalities

FINDING SLOPE

☑ The slope of a line represents the direction of a line on the coordinate plane.

☑ A coordinate plane contains two perpendicular number lines. The horizontal line is x and the vertical line is y. The point at which the two axes intersect is called the origin. An ordered pair (x, y) shows the location of a point.

☑ A line on a coordinate plane can be drawn by connecting two points.

☑ To find the slope of a line, we need the equation of the line or two points on the line.

☑ The slope of a line with two points A (x_1, y_1) and B (x_2, y_2) can be found by using this formula: $\frac{y_2 - y_1}{x_2 - x_1} = \frac{rise}{run}$

☑ The equation of a line is typically written as $y = mx + b$ where m is the slope and b is the y-intercept.

Examples:

Example 1. Find the slope of the line through these two points:

$$A(2, -7) \ and \ B(4, 3).$$

Solution: Slope $= \frac{y_2 - y_1}{x_2 - x_1}$. Let (x_1, y_1) be A$(2, -7)$ and (x_2, y_2) be $B(4, 3)$.
(Remember, you can choose any point for (x_1, y_1) and (x_2, y_2)).
Then: slope $= \frac{y_2 - y_1}{x_2 - x_1} = \frac{3 - 7}{4 - 2} = \frac{10}{2} = 5$
The slope of the line through these two points is 5.

Example 2. Find the slope of the line with equation $y = 3x + 6$

Solution: when the equation of a line is written in the form of $y = mx + b$, the slope is m. In this line: $y = 3x + 6$, the slope is 3.

GRAPHING LINES USING SLOPE–INTERCEPT FORM

Ø Slope–intercept form of a line: given the slope **m** and the **y**–intercept (the intersection of the line and y-axis) **b**, then the equation of the line is:

$$y = mx + b$$

Ø To draw the graph of a linear equation in a slope-intercept form on the xy coordinate plane, find two points on the line by plugging two values for x and calculating the values of y.

Ø You can also use the slope (m) and one point to graph the line.

Example:

Example 1. Sketch the graph of $y = 2x - 4$.

Solution: To graph this line, we need to find two points. When x is zero the value of y is -4. And when x is 2 the value of y is 0.

$$x = 0 \rightarrow y = 2(0) - 4 = -4,$$
$$y = 0 \rightarrow 0 = 2x - 4 \rightarrow x = 2$$

Now, we have two points: $(0, -4)$ and $(2, 0)$.
Find the points on the coordinate plane and graph the line. Remember that the slope of the line is 2.

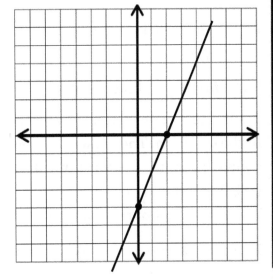

Writing Linear Equations

☒ The equation of a line in slope-intercept form: $y = mx + b$

☒ To write the equation of a line, first identify the slope.

☒ Find the y-intercept. This can be done by substituting the slope and the coordinates of a point (x, y) on the line.

Examples:

Example 1. What is the equation of the line that passes through $(2, -4)$ and has a slope of 8?

Solution: The general slope-intercept form of the equation of a line is $y = mx + b$, where m is the slope and b is the y-intercept. By substitution of the given point and given slope: $y = mx + b \rightarrow -4 = (2)(8) + b$. So, $b = -4 - 16 = -20$, and the required equation is $y = 8x - 20$

Example 2. Write the equation of the line through two points $A(2, 1)$ and $B(-2, 5)$.

Solution: First, find the slope: $Slop = \frac{y_2 - y_1}{x_2 - x_1} = \frac{5-1}{-2-2} = \frac{4}{-4} = -1 \rightarrow m = -1$

To find the value of b, use either points and plug in the values of x and y in the equation. The answer will be the same: $y = -x + b$. Let's check both points. Then: $(2, 1) \rightarrow y = mx + b \rightarrow 1 = -1(2) + b \rightarrow b = 3$
$(-2, 5) \rightarrow y = mx + b \rightarrow 5 = -1(-2) + b \rightarrow b = 3$.
The y-intercept of the line is 3. The equation of the line is: $y = -x + 3$

Example 3. What is the equation of the line that passes through $(2, -1)$ and has a slope of 5?

Solution: The general slope-intercept form of the equation of a line is $y = mx + b$, where m is the slope and b is the y-intercept. By substitution of the given point and given slope: $y = mx + b \rightarrow -1 = (5)(2) + b$
So, $b = -1 - 10 = -11$, and the equation of the line is: $y = 5x - 11$.

$= \sqrt{16 + 9} = \sqrt{25} = 5$

CHAPTER 8: PRACTICES

✍ Find the slope of each line.

1) $y = x - 3$

2) $y = -6x + 4$

3) $y = 3x - 9$

4) Line through $(-1, 3)$ and $(5, 0)$

5) Line through $(4, 0)$ and $(-2, 6)$

6) Line through $(-3, -6)$ and $(0, 3)$

✍ Sketch the graph of each line. (Using Slope–Intercept Form)

7) $y = x + 4$

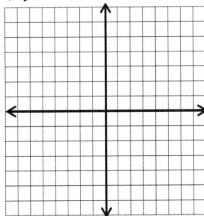

8) $y = 2x - 5$

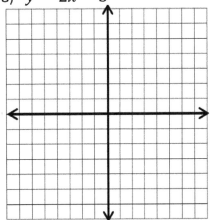

✍ Solve.

9) What is the equation of a line with slope 3 and intercept 18? _____

10) What is the equation of a line with slope 2 and passes through point $(2, 6)$?
_____

11) What is the equation of a line with slope -4 and passes through point $(-4, 8)$?
_____

12) The slope of a line is -2 and it passes through point $(-4, 3)$. What is the equation of the line? _____

13) The slope of a line is 5 and it passes through point $(-6, 3)$. What is the equation of the line? _____

✎ **Sketch the graph of each linear inequality.**

14) $y > 2x - 2$

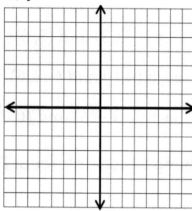

15) $y < -x + 3$

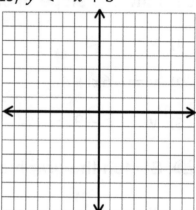

CHAPTER 8: ANSWERS

1) 1

2) -6

3) 3

4) $-\frac{1}{2}$

5) -1

6) 3

7) $y = x + 2$

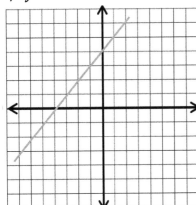

8) $y = 2x - 3$

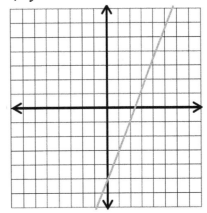

9) $y = 3x + 18$

10) $y = 2x + 2$

11) $y = -4x - 8$

12) $y = -2x - 5$

13) $y = 5x + 33$

14) $y > 2x - 2$

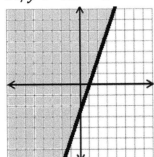

15) $y < -x + 3$

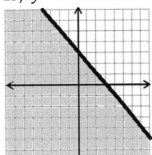

CHAPTER 9:

EXPONENTS AND VARIABLES

Math Topics that you'll learn in this chapter:

▶ Multiplication Property of Exponents

▶ Division Property of Exponents

▶ Powers of Products and Quotients

▶ Zero and Negative Exponents

▶ Negative Exponents and Negative Bases

▶ Scientific Notation

▶ Radicals

MULTIPLICATION PROPERTY OF EXPONENTS

☑ Exponents are shorthand for repeated multiplication of the same number by itself. For example, instead of 2×2, we can write 2^2. For $3 \times 3 \times 3 \times 3$, we can write 3^4

☑ In algebra, a variable is a letter used to stand for a number. The most common letters are: $x, y, z, a, b, c, m,$ and n.

☑ Exponent's rules: $x^a \times x^b = x^{a+b}$, $\frac{x^a}{x^b} = x^{a-b}$

$$(x^a)^b = x^{a \times b} \qquad\qquad (xy)^a = x^a \times y^a \qquad\qquad \left(\frac{a}{b}\right)^c = \frac{a^c}{b^c}$$

Examples:

Example 1. Multiply. $4x^3 \times 2x^2$

Solution: Use Exponent's rules: $x^a \times x^b = x^{a+b} \rightarrow x^3 \times x^2 = x^{3+2} = x^5$
Then: $4x^3 \times 2x^2 = 8x^5$

Example 2. Simplify. $\left(x^3 y^5\right)^2$

Solution: Use Exponent's rules: $(x^a)^b = x^{a \times b}$.
Then: $\left(x^3 y^5\right)^2 = x^{3 \times 2} y^{5 \times 2} = x^6 y^{10}$

Example 3. Multiply. $-2x^5 \times 7x^3$

Solution: Use Exponent's rules: $x^a \times x^b = x^{a+b} \rightarrow x^5 \times x^3 = x^{5+3} = x^8$
Then: $-2x^5 \times 7x^3 = -14x^8$

Example 4. Simplify. $(x^2 y^4)^3$

Solution: Use Exponent's rules: $(x^a)^b = x^{a \times b}$.
Then: $(x^2 y^4)^3 = x^{2 \times 3} y^{4 \times 3} = x^6 y^{12}$

DIVISION PROPERTY OF EXPONENTS

✍ Exponents are shorthand for repeated multiplication of the same number by itself. For example, instead of 3×3, we can write 3^2. For $2 \times 2 \times 2$, we can write 2^3

✍ For division of exponents use following formulas:

$$\frac{x^a}{x^b} = x^{a-b}, x \neq 0, \frac{x^a}{x^b} = \frac{1}{x^{b-a}}, x \neq 0, \qquad \frac{1}{x^b} = x^{-b}$$

Examples:

Example 1. Simplify. $\frac{12x^2y}{4xy^3} =$

Solution: First, cancel the common factor: $4 \rightarrow \frac{12x^2y}{4xy^3} = \frac{3x^2y}{xy^3}$

Use Exponent's rules: $\frac{x^a}{x^b} = x^{a-b} \rightarrow \frac{x^2}{x} = x^{2-1} = x$ and $\frac{y}{y^3} = \frac{1}{y^{3-1}} = \frac{1}{y^2}$

Then: $\frac{12x^2y}{4xy^3} = \frac{3x}{y^2}$

Example 2. Simplify. $\frac{18x^6}{2x^3} =$

Solution: Use Exponent's rules: $\frac{x^a}{x^b} = x^{b-a} \rightarrow \frac{x^6}{x^3} = x^{6-3} = x^3$

Then: $\frac{18x^6}{2x^3} = 9x^3$

Example 3. Simplify. $\frac{8x^3y}{40x^2y^3} =$

Solution: First, cancel the common factor: $8 \rightarrow \frac{8x^3y}{40x^2y^3} = \frac{x^3y}{5x^2y^3}$

Use Exponent's rules: $\frac{x^a}{x^b} = x^{a-b} \rightarrow \frac{x^3}{x^2} = x^{3-2} = x$

Then: $\frac{8x^3y}{40x^2y^3} = \frac{xy}{5y^3} \rightarrow$ now cancel the common factor: $y \rightarrow \frac{xy}{5y^3} = \frac{x}{5y^2}$

POWERS OF PRODUCTS AND QUOTIENTS

☑ Exponents are shorthand for repeated multiplication of the same number by itself. For example, instead of $2 \times 2 \times 2$, we can write 2^3. For $3 \times 3 \times 3 \times 3$, we can write 3^4

☑ For any nonzero numbers a and b and any integer x, $(ab)^x = a^x \times b^x$ and $\left(\frac{a}{b}\right)^c = \frac{a^c}{b^c}$

Examples:

Example 1. Simplify. $(6x^2y^4)^2$

Solution: Use Exponent's rules: $(x^a)^b = x^{a \times b}$
$(6x^2y^4)^2 = (6)^2(x^2)^2(y^4)^2 = 36x^{2 \times 2}y^{4 \times 2} = 36x^4y^8$

Example 2. Simplify. $\left(\frac{5x}{2x^2}\right)^2$

Solution: First, cancel the common factor: $x \rightarrow \left(\frac{5x}{2x^2}\right)^2 = \left(\frac{5}{2x}\right)^2$
Use Exponent's rules: $\left(\frac{a}{b}\right)^c = \frac{a^c}{b^c}$, Then: $\left(\frac{5}{2x}\right)^2 = \frac{5^2}{(2x)^2} = \frac{25}{4x^2}$

Example 3. Simplify. $\left(3x^5y^4\right)^2$

Solution: Use Exponent's rules: $(x^a)^b = x^{a \times b}$
$$\left(3x^5y^4\right)^2 = (3)^2\left(x^5\right)^2(y^4)^2 = 9x^{5 \times 2}y^{4 \times 2} = 9x^{10}y^8$$

Example 4. Simplify. $\left(\frac{2x}{3x^2}\right)^2$

Solution: First, cancel the common factor: $x \rightarrow \left(\frac{2x}{3x^2}\right)^2 = \left(\frac{2}{3x}\right)^2$
Use Exponent's rules: $\left(\frac{a}{b}\right)^c = \frac{a^c}{b^c}$, Then: $\left(\frac{2}{3x}\right)^2 = \frac{2^2}{(3x)^2} = \frac{4}{9x^2}$

ZERO AND NEGATIVE EXPONENTS

☑ Zero-Exponent Rule: $a^0 = 1$, this means that anything raised to the zero power is 1. For example: $(5xy)^0 = 1$

☑ A negative exponent simply means that the base is on the wrong side of the fraction line, so you need to flip the base to the other side. For instance, "x^{-2}" (pronounced as "ecks to the minus two") just means "x^2" but underneath, as in $\frac{1}{x^2}$.

Examples:

Example 1. Evaluate. $\left(\frac{2}{3}\right)^{-2} =$

Solution: Use negative exponent's rule: $\left(\frac{x^a}{x^b}\right)^{-2} = \left(\frac{x^b}{x^a}\right)^2 \rightarrow \left(\frac{2}{3}\right)^{-2} = \left(\frac{3}{2}\right)^2 =$
Then: $\left(\frac{3}{2}\right)^2 = \frac{3^2}{2^2} = \frac{9}{4}$

Example 2. Evaluate. $\left(\frac{4}{5}\right)^{-3} =$

Solution: Use negative exponent's rule: $\left(\frac{x^a}{x^b}\right)^{-2} = \left(\frac{x^b}{x^a}\right)^2 \rightarrow \left(\frac{4}{5}\right)^{-3} = \left(\frac{5}{4}\right)^3 =$
Then: $\left(\frac{5}{4}\right)^3 = \frac{5^3}{4^3} = \frac{125}{64}$

Example 3. Evaluate. $\left(\frac{x}{y}\right)^0 =$

Solution: Use zero-exponent Rule: $a^0 = 1$
Then: $\left(\frac{x}{y}\right)^0 = 1$

Example 4. Evaluate. $\left(\frac{5}{6}\right)^{-1} =$

Solution: Use negative exponent's rule: $\left(\frac{x^a}{x^b}\right)^{-2} = \left(\frac{x^b}{x^a}\right)^2 \rightarrow \left(\frac{5}{6}\right)^{-1} = \left(\frac{6}{5}\right)^1 = \frac{6}{5}$

NEGATIVE EXPONENTS AND NEGATIVE BASES

☑ A negative exponent is the reciprocal of that number with a positive exponent. $(3)^{-2} = \frac{1}{3^2}$

☑ To simplify a negative exponent, make the power positive!

☑ The parenthesis is important! -5^{-2} is not the same as $(-5)^{-2}$

$$- 5^{-2} = -\frac{1}{5^2} \text{ and } (-5)^{-2} = +\frac{1}{5^2}$$

Examples:

Example 1. Simplify. $\left(\frac{5a}{6c}\right)^{-2} =$

Solution: Use negative exponent's rule: $\left(\frac{x^a}{x^b}\right)^{-2} = \left(\frac{x^b}{x^a}\right)^2 \rightarrow \left(\frac{5a}{6c}\right)^{-2} = \left(\frac{6c}{5a}\right)^2$

Now use exponent's rule: $\left(\frac{a}{b}\right)^c = \frac{a^c}{b^c} \rightarrow = \left(\frac{6c}{5a}\right)^2 = \frac{6^2c^2}{5^2a^2}$

Then: $\frac{6^2c^2}{5^2a^2} = \frac{36c^2}{25a^2}$

Example 2. Simplify. $\left(\frac{2x}{3yz}\right)^{-3} =$

Solution: Use negative exponent's rule: $\left(\frac{x^a}{x^b}\right)^{-2} = \left(\frac{x^b}{x^a}\right)^2 \rightarrow \left(\frac{2x}{3yz}\right)^{-3} = \left(\frac{3yz}{2x}\right)^3$

Now use exponent's rule: $\left(\frac{a}{b}\right)^c = \frac{a^c}{b^c} \rightarrow \left(\frac{3yz}{2x}\right)^3 = \frac{3^3y^3z^3}{2^3x^3} = \frac{27y^3z^3}{8x^3}$

Example 3. Simplify. $\left(\frac{3a}{2c}\right)^{-2} =$

Solution: Use negative exponent's rule: $\left(\frac{x^a}{x^b}\right)^{-2} = \left(\frac{x^b}{x^a}\right)^2 \rightarrow \left(\frac{3a}{2c}\right)^{-2} = \left(\frac{2c}{3a}\right)^2$

Now use exponent's rule: $\left(\frac{a}{b}\right)^c = \frac{a^c}{b^c} \rightarrow = \left(\frac{2c}{3a}\right)^2 = \frac{2^2c^2}{3^2a^2}$

Then: $\frac{2^2c^2}{3^2a^2} = \frac{4c^2}{9a^2}$

SCIENTIFIC NOTATION

- Ø Scientific notation is used to write very big or very small numbers in decimal form.

- Ø In scientific notation, all numbers are written in the form of: $m \times 10^n$, where m is greater than 1 and less than 10.

- Ø To convert a number from scientific notation to standard form, move the decimal point to the left (if the exponent of ten is a negative number), or to the right (if the exponent is positive).

Examples:

Example 1. Write 0.00015 in scientific notation.

Solution: First, move the decimal point to the right so you have a number between 1 and 10. That number is 1.5. Now, determine how many places the decimal moved in step 1 by the power of 10. We moved the decimal point 4 digits to the right. Then: $10^{-4} \rightarrow$ When the decimal moved to the right, the exponent is negative. Then: $0.00015 = 1.5 \times 10^{-4}$

Example 2. Write 9.5×10^{-5} in standard notation.

Solution: $10^{-5} \rightarrow$ When the decimal moved to the right, the exponent is negative. Then: $9.5 \times 10^{-5} = 0.000095$

Example 3. Write 0.00012 in scientific notation.

Solution: First, move the decimal point to the right so you have a number between 1 and 10. Then: $m = 1.2$, Now, determine how many places the decimal moved in step 1 by the power of 10.
$10^{-4} \rightarrow$ Then: $0.00012 = 1.2 \times 10^{-4}$

Example 4. Write 8.3×10^5 in standard notation.
Solution: $10^{-5} \rightarrow$ The exponent is positive 5. Then, move the decimal point to the right five digits. (remember $8.3 = 8.30000$),
Then: $8.3 \times 10^5 = 830000$

RADICALS

☑ If n is a positive integer and x is a real number, then: $\sqrt[n]{x} = x^{\frac{1}{n}}$,

$$\sqrt[n]{xy} = x^{\frac{1}{n}} \times y^{\frac{1}{n}}, \ \sqrt[n]{\frac{x}{y}} = \frac{x^{\frac{1}{n}}}{y^{\frac{1}{n}}}, \text{ and } \sqrt[n]{x} \times \sqrt[n]{y} = \sqrt[n]{xy}$$

☑ A square root of x is a number r whose square is: $r^2 = x$ (r is a square root of x)

☑ To add and subtract radicals, we need to have the same values under the radical. For example: $\sqrt{3} + \sqrt{3} = 2\sqrt{3}, 3\sqrt{5} - \sqrt{5} = 2\sqrt{5}$

Examples:

Example 1. Find the square root of $\sqrt{169}$.

Solution: First, factor the number: $169 = 13^2$, Then: $\sqrt{169} = \sqrt{13^2}$, Now use radical rule: $\sqrt[n]{a^n} = a$. Then: $\sqrt{169} = \sqrt{13^2} = 13$

Example 2. Evaluate. $\sqrt{9} \times \sqrt{25} =$

Solution: Find the values of $\sqrt{9}$ and $\sqrt{25}$. Then: $\sqrt{9} \times \sqrt{25} = 3 \times 5 = 15$

Example 3. Solve. $7\sqrt{2} + 4\sqrt{2}$.

Solution: Since we have the same values under the radical, we can add these two radicals: $7\sqrt{2} + 4\sqrt{2} = 11\sqrt{2}$

Example 4. Evaluate. $\sqrt{2} \times \sqrt{8} =$

Solution: Use this radical rule: $\sqrt[n]{x} \times \sqrt[n]{y} = \sqrt[n]{xy} \rightarrow \sqrt{2} \times \sqrt{8} = \sqrt{16}$ The square root of 16 is 4. Then: $\sqrt{2} \times \sqrt{8} = \sqrt{16} = 4$

CHAPTER 9: PRACTICES

✍ Find the products.

1) $2x^3 \times 4xy^2 =$

2) $6x^2y \times 8x^2y^2 =$

3) $5x^3y^2 \times 3x^2y^3 =$

4) $7xy^4 \times 4x^2y =$

5) $3x^4y^5 \times 9x^3y^2 =$

6) $6x^3y^2 \times 7x^3y^3 =$

7) $4x^3y^6 \times 2x^4y^2 =$

8) $7x^4y^3 \times 3x^3y^2 =$

9) $10x^5y^2 \times 10x^4y^3 =$

10) $8x^2y^3 \times 5x^6y^2 =$

11) $9y^5 \times 2x^6y^3 =$

12) $7x^4 \times 7x^2y^2 =$

✍ Simplify.

13) $\dfrac{3^3 \times 3^4}{3^9 \times 3} =$

14) $\dfrac{6x}{30x^2} =$

15) $\dfrac{18x^4}{6x^3} =$

16) $\dfrac{42x^3}{56x^3y^2} =$

17) $\dfrac{18y^3}{54x^4y^4} =$

18) $\dfrac{150x^3y^5}{50x^2y^3} =$

19) $\dfrac{2^3 \times 2^2}{7^2 \times 7} =$

20) $\dfrac{12x}{2x^2} =$

21) $\dfrac{25x^6}{5x^3} =$

22) $\dfrac{48y^4}{56x^5y^3} =$

✍ Solve.

23) $(3x^2y^6)^3 =$

24) $(2x^3y^4)^5 =$

25) $(2x \times 5xy^2)^2 =$

26) $(3x \times 2y^3)^2 =$

27) $\left(\dfrac{8x}{x^3}\right)^3 =$

28) $\left(\dfrac{9y}{3y^2}\right)^3 =$

29) $\left(\dfrac{6x^3y^4}{2x^4y^2}\right)^3 =$

30) $\left(\dfrac{27x^4y^4}{54x^3y^5}\right)^2 =$

31) $\left(\dfrac{9x^8y^4}{3x^5y^2}\right)^2 =$

32) $\left(\dfrac{35x^7y^4}{7x^5y^3}\right)^2 =$

✍ Evaluate each expression. (Zero and Negative Exponents)

33) $\left(\frac{1}{8}\right)^{-3} =$

34) $\left(\frac{1}{6}\right)^{-2} =$

35) $\left(\frac{3}{4}\right)^{-2} =$

36) $\left(\frac{4}{9}\right)^{-2} =$

37) $\left(\frac{1}{4}\right)^{-4} =$

38) $\left(\frac{2}{7}\right)^{-3} =$

✍ Write each expression with positive exponents.

39) $18x^{-2}y^{-6} =$

40) $35x^{-3}y^{-5} =$

41) $-12y^{-4} =$

42) $-25x^{-6} =$

43) $15a^{-3}b^6 =$

44) $20a^6b^{-5}c^{-3} =$

45) $46x^6y^{-3}z^{-7} =$

46) $\frac{16y}{x^3y^{-3}} =$

47) $\frac{24a^{-3}b}{-16c^{-3}}$

✍ Write each number in scientific notation.

48) $0.00521 =$

49) $0.000067 =$

50) $25,000 =$

51) $36,000,000 =$

✍ Evaluate.

52) $\sqrt{6} \times \sqrt{6} =$ ....

53) $\sqrt{49} - \sqrt{4} =$ ....

54) $\sqrt{36} + \sqrt{64} =$ ....

55) $\sqrt{9} \times \sqrt{49} =$ ....

56) $\sqrt{2} \times \sqrt{18} =$ ....

57) $3\sqrt{5} + 2\sqrt{5} =$ ....

CHAPTER 9: ANSWERS

1) $8x^4y^2$

2) $48x^4y^3$

3) $15x^5y^5$

4) $28x^3y^5$

5) $27x^7y^7$

6) $42x^6y^5$

7) $8x^7y^8$

8) $21x^7y^5$

9) $100x^9y^5$

10) $40x^8y^5$

11) $18x^6y^8$

12) $49x^6y^2$

13) $\frac{1}{27}$

14) $\frac{1}{5x}$

15) $3x$

16) $\frac{3}{4y^2}$

17) $\frac{1}{3x^4y}$

18) $3xy^2$

19) $\frac{32}{343}$

20) $\frac{6}{x}$

21) $5x^3$

22) $\frac{6y}{7x^5}$

23) $27x^6y^{18}$

24) $32x^{15}y^{20}$

25) $100x^4y^4$

26) $36x^2y^6$

27) $\frac{512}{x^6}$

28) $\frac{27}{y^3}$

29) $\frac{27y^6}{x^3}$

30) $\frac{x^2}{4y^2}$

31) $9x^6y^4$

32) $25x^4y^2$

33) 512

34) 36

35) $\frac{16}{9}$

36) $\frac{81}{16}$

37) 256

38) $\frac{343}{8}$

39) $\frac{18}{x^2y^6}$

40) $\frac{35}{x^3y^5}$

41) $-\frac{12}{y^4}$

42) $-\frac{25}{x^6}$

43) $\frac{15b^6}{a^3}$

44) $\frac{20a^6}{b^5c^3}$

45) $\frac{46x^6}{y^3z^7}$

46) $\frac{16y^4}{x^3}$

47) $-\frac{3bc^3}{2a^3}$

48) 5.21×10^{-3}

49) 6.7×10^{-5}

50) 25×10^3

51) 36×10^6

52) 6

53) 5

54) 14

55) 21

56) 6

57) $5\sqrt{5}$

CHAPTER 10:

GEOMETRY AND SOLID FIGURES

Math Topics that you'll learn in this chapter:

▶ The Pythagorean Theorem

▶ Triangles

▶ Polygons

▶ Circles

▶ Trapezoids

▶ Cubes

▶ Rectangle Prisms

▶ Cylinder

THE PYTHAGOREAN THEOREM

☒ You can use the Pythagorean Theorem to find a missing side in a right triangle.

☒ In any right triangle: $a^2 + b^2 = c^2$

Examples:

Example 1. Right triangle ABC (not shown) has two legs of lengths 6 cm (AB) and 8 cm (AC). What is the length of the hypotenuse of the triangle (side BC)?

Solution: Use Pythagorean Theorem: $a^2 + b^2 = c^2$, $a = 6$, and $b = 8$
Then: $a^2 + b^2 = c^2 \rightarrow 6^2 + 8^2 = c^2 \rightarrow 36 + 64 = c^2 \rightarrow 100 = c^2 \rightarrow c = \sqrt{100} = 10$
The length of the hypotenuse is 10 cm.

Example 2. Find the hypotenuse of this triangle.

Solution: Use Pythagorean Theorem: $a^2 + b^2 = c^2$
Then: $a^2 + b^2 = c^2 \rightarrow 12^2 + 5^2 = c^2 \rightarrow 144 + 25 = c^2$
$c^2 = 169 \rightarrow c = \sqrt{169} = 13$

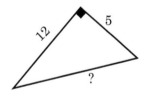

Example 3. Find the length of the missing side in this triangle.

Solution: Use Pythagorean Theorem: $a^2 + b^2 = c^2$
Then: $a^2 + b^2 = c^2 \rightarrow 3^2 + b^2 = 5^2 \rightarrow 9 + b^2 = 25 \rightarrow$
$b^2 = 25 - 9 \rightarrow b^2 = 16 \rightarrow b = \sqrt{16} = 4$

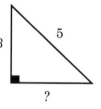

TRIANGLES

☑ In any triangle, the sum of all angles is 180 degrees.

☑ Area of a triangle $= \frac{1}{2}$ ($base \times height$)

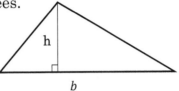

Examples:

What is the area of the following triangles?

Example 1.

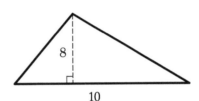

Solution: Use the area formula:

Area $= \frac{1}{2}$ ($base \times height$)

$base = 10$ and $height = 8$

Area $= \frac{1}{2}(10 \times 8) = \frac{1}{2}(80) = 40$

Example 2.

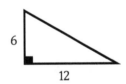

Solution: Use the area formula:

Area $= \frac{1}{2}$ ($base \times height$)

$base = 12$ and $height = 6$; Area $= \frac{1}{2}(12 \times 6) = \frac{72}{2} = 36$

Example 3. What is the missing angle in this triangle?

Solution:

In any triangle, the sum of all angles is 180 degrees. Let x be the missing angle.

Then: $50 + 85 + x = 180$;

$\rightarrow 135 + x = 180 \rightarrow x = 180 - 135 = 45$

The missing angle is 45 degrees.

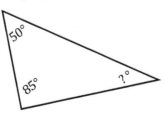

POLYGONS

☑ The perimeter of a square $= 4 \times side = 4s$

☑ The perimeter of a rectangle $= 2(width + length)$

☑ The perimeter of trapezoid $= a + b + c + d$

☑ The perimeter of a regular hexagon $= 6a$

☑ The perimeter of a parallelogram $= 2(l + w)$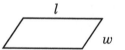

Examples:

Example 1. Find the perimeter of following regular hexagon.

Solution: Since the hexagon is regular, all sides are equal.
Then: The perimeter of The hexagon $= 6 \times (one\ side)$
The perimeter of The hexagon $= 6 \times (one\ side) = 6 \times 4 = 24\ m$

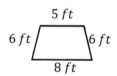

Example 2. Find the perimeter of following trapezoid.

Solution: The perimeter of a trapezoid $= a + b + c + d$
The perimeter of the trapezoid $= 5 + 6 + 6 + 8 = 25\ ft$

CIRCLES

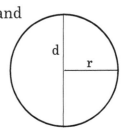

☑ In a circle, variable r is usually used for the radius and d for diameter.

☑ *Area of a circle* $= \pi r^2$ (π is about 3.14)

☑ *Circumference of a circle* $= 2\pi r$

Examples:

Example 1. Find the area of this circle.

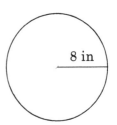

Solution:
Use area formula: $Area = \pi r^2$
$r = 8 \, in \rightarrow Area = \pi(8)^2 = 64\pi$, $\pi = 3.14$
Then: $Area = 64 \times 3.14 = 200.96 \, in^2$

Example 2. Find the Circumference of this circle.

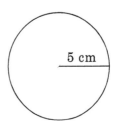

Solution:
Use Circumference formula: $Circumference = 2\pi r$
$r = 5 \, cm \rightarrow Circumference = 2\pi(5) = 10\pi$
$\pi = 3.14$ Then: $Circumference = 10 \times 3.14 = 31.4 \, cm$

Example 3. Find the area of the circle.

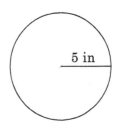

Solution:
Use area formula: $Area = \pi r^2$,
$r = 5 \, in$ then: $Area = \pi(5)^2 = 25\pi$, $\pi = 3.14$
Then: $Area = 25 \times 3.14 = 78.5$

TRAPEZOIDS

☑ A quadrilateral with at least one pair of parallel sides is a trapezoid.

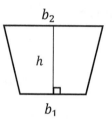

☑ Area of a trapezoid $= \frac{1}{2}h(b_1 + b_2)$

Examples:

Example 1. Calculate the area of this trapezoid.

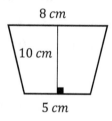

Solution:

Use area formula: $A = \frac{1}{2}h(b_1 + b_2)$

$b_1 = 5\ cm$, $b_2 = 8\ cm$ and $h = 10\ cm$

Then: $A = \frac{1}{2}(10)(8 + 5) = 5(13) = 65\ cm^2$

Example 2. Calculate the area of this trapezoid.

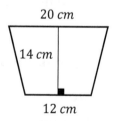

Solution:

Use area formula: $A = \frac{1}{2}h(b_1 + b_2)$

$b_1 = 12\ cm$, $b_2 = 20\ cm$ and $h = 14\ cm$

Then: $A = \frac{1}{2}(14)(12 + 20) = 7(32) = 224\ cm^2$

CUBES

☑ A cube is a three-dimensional solid object bounded by six square sides.

☑ Volume is the measure of the amount of space inside of a solid figure, like a cube, ball, cylinder or pyramid.

☑ The volume of a cube $= (one\ side)^3$

☑ The surface area of a cube $= 6 \times (one\ side)^2$

Examples:

Example 1. Find the volume and surface area of this cube.

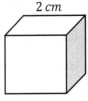

Solution: Use volume formula: $volume = (one\ side)^3$
Then: $volume = (one\ side)^3 = (2)^3 = 8\ cm^3$
Use surface area formula:
$surface\ area\ of\ cube: 6(one\ side)^2 = 6(2)^2 = 6(4) = 24\ cm^2$

Example 2. Find the volume and surface area of this cube.

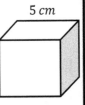

Solution: Use volume formula: $volume = (one\ side)^3$
Then: $volume = (one\ side)^3 = (5)^3 = 125\ cm^3$
Use surface area formula:
$surface\ area\ of\ cube: 6(one\ side)^2 = 6(5)^2 = 6(25) = 150\ cm^2$

Example 3. Find the volume and surface area of this cube.

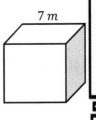

Solution: Use volume formula: $volume = (one\ side)^3$
Then: $volume = (one\ side)^3 = (7)^3 = 343\ m^3$
Use surface area formula:
$surface\ area\ of\ cube: 6(one\ side)^2 = 6(7)^2 = 6(49) = 294\ m^2$

RECTANGULAR PRISMS

☑ A rectangular prism is a solid 3-dimensional object with six rectangular faces.

☑ The volume of a Rectangular prism = *Length × Width × Height*

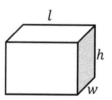

$Volume = l \times w \times h$

$Surface\ area = 2 \times (wh + lw + lh)$

Examples:

Example 1. Find the volume and surface area of this rectangular prism.

Solution: Use volume formula: $Volume = l \times w \times h$
Then: $Volume = 8 \times 6 \times 10 = 480\ m^3$
Use surface area formula: $Surface\ area = 2 \times (wh + lw + lh)$
Then: $Surface\ area = 2 \times \big((6 \times 10) + (8 \times 6) + (8 \times 10)\big)$
$$= 2 \times (60 + 48 + 80) = 2 \times (188) = 376\ m^2$$

Example 2. Find the volume and surface area of this rectangular prism.

Solution: Use volume formula: $Volume = l \times w \times h$
Then: $Volume = 10 \times 8 \times 12 = 960\ m^3$
Use surface area formula: $Surface\ area = 2 \times (wh + lw + lh)$
Then: $Surface\ area = 2 \times \big((8 \times 12) + (10 \times 8) + (10 \times 12)\big)$
$$= 2 \times (96 + 80 + 120) = 2 \times (296) = 592\ m^2$$

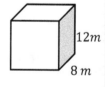

CYLINDER

☑ A cylinder is a solid geometric figure with straight parallel sides and a circular or oval cross-section.

☑ *Volume of a Cylinder* $= \pi(radius)^2 \times height$, $\pi \approx 3.14$

☑ *Surface area of a cylinder* $= 2\pi r^2 + 2\pi rh$

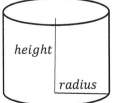

Examples:

Example 1. Find the volume and Surface area of the follow Cylinder.

Solution: Use volume formula:
$Volume = \pi(radius)^2 \times height$
Then: $Volume = \pi(3)^2 \times 8 = 9\pi \times 8 = 72\pi$
$\pi = 3.14$ then: $Volume = 72\pi = 72 \times 3.14 = 226.08\ cm^3$
Use surface area formula: $Surface\ area = 2\pi r^2 + 2\pi rh$
Then: $2\pi(3)^2 + 2\pi(3)(8) = 2\pi(9) + 2\pi(24) = 18\pi + 48\pi = 66\pi$
$\pi = 3.14$ Then: $Surface\ area = 66 \times 3.14 = 207.24\ cm^2$

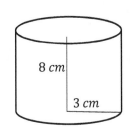

Example 2. Find the volume and Surface area of the follow Cylinder.

Solution: Use volume formula:
$Volume = \pi(radius)^2 \times height$
Then: $Volume = \pi(2)^2 \times 6 = \pi 4 \times 6 = 24\pi$
$\pi = 3.14$ then: $Volume = 24\pi = 75.36\ cm^3$
Use surface area formula: $Surface\ area = 2\pi r^2 + 2\pi rh$
Then: $= 2\pi(2)^2 + 2\pi(2)(6) = 2\pi(4) + 2\pi(12) = 8\pi + 24\pi = 32\pi$
$\pi = 3.14$ then: $Surface\ area = 32 \times 3.14 = 100.48\ cm^2$

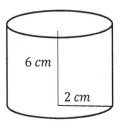

CHAPTER 10: PRACTICES

🖎 Find the missing side?

1)
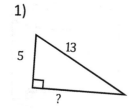

2)
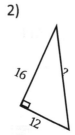

3)
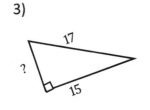

4)
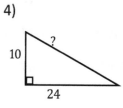

🖎 Find the measure of the unknown angle in each triangle.

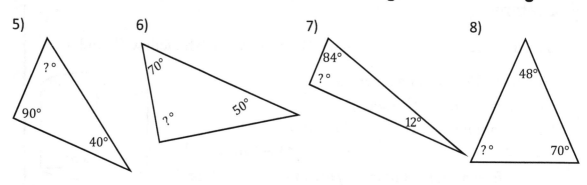

5) 6) 7) 8)

🖎 Find the area of each triangle.

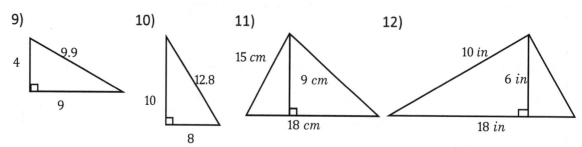

9) 10) 11) 12)

🖎 Find the perimeter or circumference of each shape.

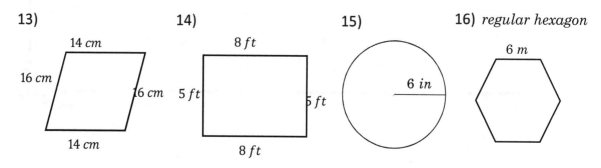

13) 14) 15) 16) *regular hexagon*

🖎 **Find the area of each trapezoid.**

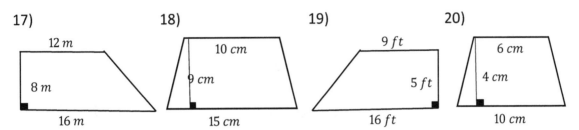

17)
12 m
8 m
16 m

18)
10 cm
9 cm
15 cm

19)
9 ft
5 ft
16 ft

20)
6 cm
4 cm
10 cm

🖎 **Find the volume of each cube.**

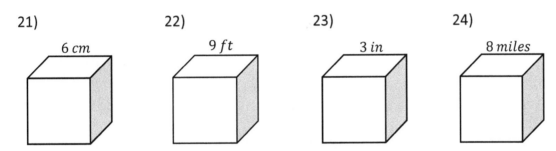

21)
6 cm

22)
9 ft

23)
3 in

24)
8 miles

🖎 **Find the volume of each Rectangular Prism.**

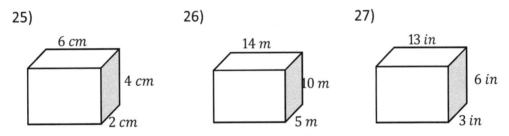

25)
6 cm
4 cm
2 cm

26)
14 m
10 m
5 m

27)
13 in
6 in
3 in

🖎 **Find the volume of each Cylinder. Round your answer to the nearest tenth. ($\pi = 3.14$)**

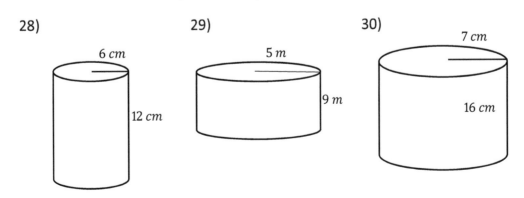

28)
6 cm
12 cm

29)
5 m
9 m

30)
7 cm
16 cm

CHAPTER 10: ANSWERS

1) 12

2) 20

3) 8

4) 26

5) 50

6) 60

7) 84

8) 62

9) 18

10) 40

11) $81\ cm^2$

12) $54 in^2$

13) $60\ cm$

14) $26\ ft$

15) $12\ \pi \approx 37.68\ in$

16) $36\ m$

17) $112\ m^2$

18) $112.5\ cm^2$

19) $62.5\ ft^2$

20) $32\ cm^2$

21) $216\ cm^3$

22) $729\ ft^3$

23) $27\ in^3$

24) $512\ mi^3$

25) $48\ cm^3$

26) $700\ m^3$

27) $234\ in^3$

28) $1,356.5\ cm^3$

29) $706.5\ m^3$

30) $2,461.8\ cm^3$

CHAPTER 11:

STATISTICS

Math Topics that you'll learn in this chapter:

▶ Mean, Median, Mode, and Range of the Given Data

▶ Pie Graph

▶ Probability Problems

▶ Permutations and Combinations

MEAN, MEDIAN, MODE, AND RANGE OF THE GIVEN DATA

- ☑ Mean: $\dfrac{sum\ of\ the\ data}{total\ number\ of\ data\ entires}$

- ☑ Mode: the value in the list that appears most often

- ☑ Median: is the middle number of a group of numbers arranged in order by size.

- ☑ Range: the difference of the largest value and smallest value in the list

Examples:

Example 1. What is the mode of these numbers? $4, 5, 7, 5, 7, 4, 0, 4$

Solution: Mode: the value in the list that appears most often. Therefore, the mode is number 4. There are three number 4 in the data.

Example 2. What is the median of these numbers? $5, 10, 14, 9, 16, 19, 6$

Solution: Write the numbers in order: $5, 6, 9, 10, 14, 16, 19$
The median is the number in the middle. Therefore, the median is 10.

Example 3. What is the mean of these numbers? $8, 2, 8, 5, 3, 2, 4, 8$

Solution: Mean: $\dfrac{sum\ of\ the\ data}{total\ number\ of\ data\ entires} = \dfrac{8+2+8+5+3+2+4+8}{8} = 5$

Example 4. What is the range in this list? $4, 9, 13, 8, 15, 18, 5$

Solution: Range is the difference of the largest value and smallest value in the list. The largest value is 18 and the smallest value is 4.
Then: $18 - 4 = 14$

PIE GRAPH

☑ A Pie Chart is a circle chart divided into sectors, each sector represents the relative size of each value.

☑ Pie charts represent a snapshot of how a group is broken down into smaller pieces.

Example:

A library has 820 books that include Mathematics, Physics, Chemistry, English and History. Use the following graph to answer the questions.

Example 1. What is the number of Mathematics books?

Solution: Number of total books = 820

Percent of Mathematics books = 30% = 0.30

Then, the number of Mathematics books: $0.30 \times 820 = 246$

Example 2. What is the number of History books?

Solution: Number of total books = 820

Percent of History books = 10% = 0.10

Then: $0.10 \times 820 = 82$

Example 3. What is the number of Chemistry books?

Solution: Number of total books = 820

Percent of Chemistry books = 20% = 0.20

Then: $0.20 \times 820 = 164$

PROBABILITY PROBLEMS

☑ Probability is the likelihood of something happening in the future. It is expressed as a number between zero (can never happen) to 1 (will always happen).

☑ Probability can be expressed as a fraction, a decimal, or a percent.

☑ Probability formula: $Probability = \frac{number\ of\ desired\ outcomes}{number\ of\ total\ outcomes}$

Examples:

Example 1. Anita's trick–or–treat bag contains 12 pieces of chocolate, 18 suckers, 18 pieces of gum, 24 pieces of licorice. If she randomly pulls a piece of candy from her bag, what is the probability of her pulling out a piece of sucker?

Solution: Probability $= \frac{number\ of\ desired\ outcomes}{number\ of\ total\ outcomes}$

Probability of pulling out a piece of sucker $= \frac{18}{12 + 18 + 18 + 24} = \frac{18}{72} = \frac{1}{4}$

Example 2. A bag contains 20 balls: four green, five black, eight blue, a brown, a red and one white. If 19 balls are removed from the bag at random, what is the probability that a brown ball has been removed?

Solution: If 19 balls are removed from the bag at random, there will be one ball in the bag. The probability of choosing a brown ball is 1 out of 20. Therefore, the probability of not choosing a brown ball is 19 out of 20 and the probability of having not a brown ball after removing 19 balls is the same.

PERMUTATIONS AND COMBINATIONS

☑ Factorials are products, indicated by an exclamation mark. For example, $4! = 4 \times 3 \times 2 \times 1$ (Remember that $0!$ is defined to be equal to 1.)

☑ Permutations: The number of ways to choose a sample of k elements from a set of n distinct objects where order does matter, and replacements are not allowed. For a permutation problem, use this formula:

$$_n\mathrm{Pk} = \frac{n!}{(n-k)!}$$

☑ Combination: The number of ways to choose a sample of r elements from a set of n distinct objects where order does not matter, and replacements are not allowed. For a combination problem, use this formula:

$$_n\mathrm{Cr} = \frac{n!}{r!\,(n-r)!}$$

Examples:

Example 1. How many ways can the first and second place be awarded to 8 people?

Solution: Since the order matters, (the first and second place are different!) we need to use permutation formula where n is 10 and k is 2. Then: $\frac{n!}{(n-k)!} = \frac{8!}{(8-2)!} = \frac{8!}{6!} = \frac{8 \times 7 \times 6!}{6!}$, remove 6! from both sides of the fraction. Then: $\frac{8 \times 7 \times 6!}{6!} = 8 \times 7 = 56$

Example 2. How many ways can we pick a team of 2 people from a group of 6?

Solution: Since the order doesn't matter, we need to use a combination formula where n is 8 and r is 3. Then: $\frac{n!}{r!\,(n-r)!} = \frac{6!}{2!\,(6-2)!} = \frac{6!}{2!\,(4)!} = \frac{6 \times 5 \times 4!}{2!\,(4)!} = \frac{6 \times 5}{2 \times 1} = \frac{30}{2} = 15$

CHAPTER 11: PRACTICES

✑ **Find the values of the Given Data.**

1) 7, 10, 4, 2, 7

    Mode: _____   Range: _____

    Mean: _____   Median: _____

2) 4, 8, 2, 9, 8, 5

    Mode: _____   Range: _____

    Mean: _____   Median: _____

3) 12, 2, 6, 10, 6, 15

    Mode: _____   Range: _____

    Mean: _____   Median: _____

4) 12, 5, 1, 10, 2, 11, 1

    Mode: _____   Range: _____

    Mean: _____   Median: _____

✑ **The circle graph below shows all Bob's expenses for last month. Bob spent $896 on his Rent last month.**

5) How much did Bob's total expenses last month? _____

6) How much did Bob spend for foods last month? _____

7) How much did Bob spend for his bills last month? _____

8) How much did Bob spend on his car last month? _____

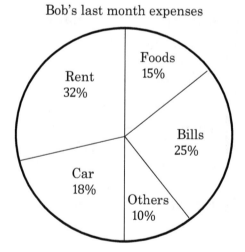

Bob's last month expenses

✎ Solve.

9) Bag A contains 6 red marbles and 9 green marbles. Bag B contains 4 black marbles and 7 orange marbles. What is the probability of selecting a green marble at random from bag A? What is the probability of selecting a black marble at random from Bag B?

_____   _____

✎ Solve.

10) Susan is baking cookies. She uses sugar, flour, butter, and eggs. How many different orders of ingredients can she try? _____

11) Jason is planning for his vacation. He wants to go to museum, go to the beach, and play volleyball. How many different ways of ordering are there for him? _____

12) In how many ways can a team of 8 basketball players choose a captain and co-captain? _____

13) How many ways can you give 6 balls to your 8 friends? _____

14) A professor is going to arrange her 6 students in a straight line. In how many ways can she do this? _____

15) In how many ways can a teacher chooses 5 out of 13 students? _____

CHAPTER 11: ANSWERS

1) Mode: 7, Range: 8, Mean: 6, Median: 7

2) Mode: 8, Range:7, Mean: 6, Median: 6.5

3) Mode: 6, Range: 13, Mean: 8.5, Median: 8

4) Mode: 1, Range: 11, Mean: 19.5, Median: 6

5) $2,800

6) $420

7) $700

8) $504

9) $\frac{3}{5}, \frac{4}{11}$

10) 24

11) 6

12) 56 (it's a permutation problem)

13) 28 (it's a combination problem)

14) 720

15) 1,287 (it's a combination problem)

SSAT MIDDLE LEVEL TEST REVIEW

The SSAT, or Secondary School Admissions Test, is a standardized test to help determine admission to private elementary, middle and high schools.

There are currently three Levels of the SSAT:

- ❖ Lower Level (for students in 3rd and 4th grade)
- ❖ Middle Level (for students in 5th-7th grade)
- ❖ Upper Level (for students in 8th-11th grade)

There are six sections on the SSAT Middle Level Test:

- ❖ Writing: 25 minutes.
- ❖ Math section: 25 questions, 30 minutes
- ❖ Reading section: 40 questions, 40 minutes
- ❖ Verbal section: 60 questions, 30 minutes
- ❖ Math section: 25 questions, 30 minutes
- ❖ Experimental: 16 questions, 15 minutes.

In this book, there are 2 complete SSAT Middle Level Math Practice Tests. Take these tests to see what score you'll be able to receive on a real SSAT Middle Level test.

Good luck!

Time to refine your skill with a practice examination

Take a practice SSAT Middle Level Mathematics Test to simulate the test day experience. After you've finished, score your test using the answer keys.

Before You Start

- ❖ You'll need a pencil and a timer to take the test.
- ❖ Each test contains 25 multiple-choice questions. For each question, there are five possible answers. Choose which one is best.
- ❖ After you've finished the test, review the answer key to see where you went wrong.
- ❖ Use the answer sheet provided to record your answers. (You can cut it out or photocopy it)
- ❖ You will receive 1 point for every correct answer, and you will lose $\frac{1}{4}$ point for each incorrect answer. There is no penalty for skipping a question.

Calculators are NOT permitted for the SSAT Middle Level Test

Good Luck!

SSAT MIDDLE LEVEL MATH PRACTICE TEST 1

2023 - 2024

Two Parts

▶ **Total number of questions:** 50
▶ **Section 1:** 25 questions
▶ **Section 2:** 25 questions
▶ **Total time for two parts:** 60 Minutes

SSAT Middle Level Practice Tests Answer Sheet

Remove (or photocopy) these answer sheets and use them to complete the practice tests.

SSAT Middle Level Mathematics Practice Test 3 Answer Sheet

SSAT Middle Level Practice Test 1 Section 1

#		#		#	
1	Ⓐ Ⓑ Ⓒ Ⓓ Ⓔ	11	Ⓐ Ⓑ Ⓒ Ⓓ Ⓔ	21	Ⓐ Ⓑ Ⓒ Ⓓ Ⓔ
2	Ⓐ Ⓑ Ⓒ Ⓓ Ⓔ	12	Ⓐ Ⓑ Ⓒ Ⓓ Ⓔ	22	Ⓐ Ⓑ Ⓒ Ⓓ Ⓔ
3	Ⓐ Ⓑ Ⓒ Ⓓ Ⓔ	13	Ⓐ Ⓑ Ⓒ Ⓓ Ⓔ	23	Ⓐ Ⓑ Ⓒ Ⓓ Ⓔ
4	Ⓐ Ⓑ Ⓒ Ⓓ Ⓔ	14	Ⓐ Ⓑ Ⓒ Ⓓ Ⓔ	24	Ⓐ Ⓑ Ⓒ Ⓓ Ⓔ
5	Ⓐ Ⓑ Ⓒ Ⓓ Ⓔ	15	Ⓐ Ⓑ Ⓒ Ⓓ Ⓔ	25	Ⓐ Ⓑ Ⓒ Ⓓ Ⓔ
6	Ⓐ Ⓑ Ⓒ Ⓓ Ⓔ	16	Ⓐ Ⓑ Ⓒ Ⓓ Ⓔ		
7	Ⓐ Ⓑ Ⓒ Ⓓ Ⓔ	17	Ⓐ Ⓑ Ⓒ Ⓓ Ⓔ		
8	Ⓐ Ⓑ Ⓒ Ⓓ Ⓔ	18	Ⓐ Ⓑ Ⓒ Ⓓ Ⓔ		
9	Ⓐ Ⓑ Ⓒ Ⓓ Ⓔ	19	Ⓐ Ⓑ Ⓒ Ⓓ Ⓔ		
10	Ⓐ Ⓑ Ⓒ Ⓓ Ⓔ	20	Ⓐ Ⓑ Ⓒ Ⓓ Ⓔ		

SSAT Middle Level Practice Test 1 Section 2

#		#		#	
1	Ⓐ Ⓑ Ⓒ Ⓓ Ⓔ	11	Ⓐ Ⓑ Ⓒ Ⓓ Ⓔ	21	Ⓐ Ⓑ Ⓒ Ⓓ Ⓔ
2	Ⓐ Ⓑ Ⓒ Ⓓ Ⓔ	12	Ⓐ Ⓑ Ⓒ Ⓓ Ⓔ	22	Ⓐ Ⓑ Ⓒ Ⓓ Ⓔ
3	Ⓐ Ⓑ Ⓒ Ⓓ Ⓔ	13	Ⓐ Ⓑ Ⓒ Ⓓ Ⓔ	23	Ⓐ Ⓑ Ⓒ Ⓓ Ⓔ
4	Ⓐ Ⓑ Ⓒ Ⓓ Ⓔ	14	Ⓐ Ⓑ Ⓒ Ⓓ Ⓔ	24	Ⓐ Ⓑ Ⓒ Ⓓ Ⓔ
5	Ⓐ Ⓑ Ⓒ Ⓓ Ⓔ	15	Ⓐ Ⓑ Ⓒ Ⓓ Ⓔ	25	Ⓐ Ⓑ Ⓒ Ⓓ Ⓔ
6	Ⓐ Ⓑ Ⓒ Ⓓ Ⓔ	16	Ⓐ Ⓑ Ⓒ Ⓓ Ⓔ		
7	Ⓐ Ⓑ Ⓒ Ⓓ Ⓔ	17	Ⓐ Ⓑ Ⓒ Ⓓ Ⓔ		
8	Ⓐ Ⓑ Ⓒ Ⓓ Ⓔ	18	Ⓐ Ⓑ Ⓒ Ⓓ Ⓔ		
9	Ⓐ Ⓑ Ⓒ Ⓓ Ⓔ	19	Ⓐ Ⓑ Ⓒ Ⓓ Ⓔ		
10	Ⓐ Ⓑ Ⓒ Ⓓ Ⓔ	20	Ⓐ Ⓑ Ⓒ Ⓓ Ⓔ		

SSAT Middle Level Math Practice Test 1 Section 1

Total number of questions: 25

Total time for this section: 30 Minutes

You may NOT use a calculator on this part.

1) If 30 percent of a number is 180, then 12 percent of the same number is

A. 60

B. 72

C. 80

D. 90

E. 120

2) If 0.45 equals $4.5F$, what is the value of $10F$?

A. 0.01

B. 0.1

C. 1.0

D. 1.01

E. 1.001

3) Nicole borrowed $5,800 for three months at an annual rate of 4%. How much interest did Nicole owe?

A. $45

B. $58

C. $116

D. $232

E. $480

4) If three times a certain number, increased by 6, is equal to 30, what is the number?

A. 8

B. 12

C. 20

D. 28

E. 54

5) How long does a 320–miles trip take moving at 50 miles per hour (*mph*)?

A. 6 *hours*

B. 6 *hours and* 24 *minutes*

C. 6 *hours and* 44 *minutes*

D. 7 *hours and* 34 *minutes*

E. 10 *hours and* 24 *minutes*

6) The marked price of a computer is D dollar. Its price decreased by 15% in January and later increased by 15% in February. What is the final price of the computer in D dollar?

A. 0.80 D

B. 0.88 D

C. 0.97 D

D. 1.20 D

E. 1.40 D

7) The average of $14, 16, 21$ and x is 20. What is the value of x?

A. 10

B. 16

C. 18

D. 20

E. 29

8) What is the value of x in the following equation?
$$\frac{x+4}{2} = 6$$

A. 2

B. 4

C. 8

D. 9

E. 10

9) John has M toy cars. Jack has 5 more cars than John. If Jack gives John 2 cars, how many cars will Jack have, in terms of M?

A. M

B. $M - 1$

C. $M + 1$

D. $M + 3$

E. $M + 4$

10) If 12% of A is 3% of B, then B is what percent of A?

A. 3%

B. 30%

C. 200%

D. 300%

E. 400%

11) The ratio of boys to girls in a school is 3:2. If there are 600 students in a school, how many boys are in the school.

A. 540

B. 450

C. 360

D. 290

E. 240

12) In five successive hours, a car traveled 41 km, 46 km, 52 km, 36 km and 51 km. In the next five hours, it traveled with an average speed of 60 km per $hour$. Find the total distance the car traveled in 10 hours.

A. 420 km

B. 456 km

C. 475 km

D. 526 km

E. 1,000 km

13) Two third of 45 is equal to $\frac{4}{5}$ of what number?

A. 25

B. 37.5

C. 40

D. 42.5

E. 450

14) What is the cost of six ounces of cheese at $0.80 per $pound$?

A. $0.30

B. $0.44

C. $0.48

D. $0.52

E. $0.87

15) If 30% of a class are girls, and 20% of girls play tennis, what percent of the class play tennis?

A. 6%

B. 10%

C. 15%

D. 30%

E. 40%

16) Sophia purchased a sofa for $414.00. The sofa is regularly priced at $600.00. What was the percent discount Sophia received on the sofa?

A. 12%

B. 15%

C. 20%

D. 25%

E. 31%

17) When a number is subtracted from 36 and the difference is divided by that number, the result is 3. What is the value of the number?

A. 3

B. 4

C. 9

D. 12

E. 25

18) 50 students took an exam and 12 of them failed. What percent of the students passed the exam?

A. 30%

B. 40%

C. 76%

D. 80%

E. 90%

19) What is the value of x in the following equation?
$$3x + 10 = 46$$

A. 4

B. 7

C. 10

D. 11

E. 12

20) A bag contains 19 balls: three green, five black, eight blue, a brown, a red and one white. If 18 balls are removed from the bag at random, what is the probability that a brown ball has been removed?

A. $\frac{1}{9}$

B. $\frac{1}{7}$

C. $\frac{16}{19}$

D. $\frac{18}{19}$

E. $\frac{1}{2}$

21) If $M \times \frac{4}{3} \times 4 = 1$, then $M =$....

A. $\frac{3}{16}$

B. $\frac{4}{16}$

C. 1

D. 1.2

E. 4

22) Ava left a $4.50 tip on a lunch that cost $30.00, approximately what percentage was the tip?

A. 25%

B. 22%

C. 20%

D. 18%

E. 15%

23) In 1989, the average worker's income increased $3,000 per year starting from $25,000 annual salary. Which equation represents income greater than average? (I = income, x = number of years after 1989)

A. $I > 3,000x + 25,000$

B. $I > -3,000x + 25,000$

C. $I < -3,000x + 25,000$

D. $I < 3,000x - 25,000$

E. $I < 25,000x + 25,000$

24) If 50% of a number is 5, what is the number?

A. 4

B. 8

C. 10

D. 20

E. 25

25) If $\frac{z}{5} = 4$, then $z + 5 = ?$

A. 4

B. 5

C. 15

D. 20

E. 25

IF YOU FINISH BEFORE TIME IS CALLED, YOU MAY CHECK YOUR WORK ON THIS SECTION ONLY. DO NOT TURN TO ANY OTHER SECTION IN THE TEST. **STOP**

.... www.EffortlessMath.com

SSAT Middle Level Math Practice Test 1 Section 2

Total number of questions: 25

Total time for this section: 30 Minutes

You may NOT use a calculator on this part.

1) If $(10 - 5) \times 4 = 10 + \square$, then $\square$=?

A. 4

B. 5

C. 7

D. 8

E. 10

2) What is the value of x in this equation?
$$\frac{x - 3}{5} + 5 = 20$$

A. 131

B. 128

C. 115

D. 100

E. 78

3) A bank is offering 5.5% simple interest on a savings account. If you deposit $7,000, how much interest will you earn in five years?

A. $360

B. $720

C. $1,925

D. $2,600

E. $4,800

4) Emma needs an 75% average in her writing class to pass. On her first 4 exams, she earned scores of 68%, 75%, 80%, and 90%. What is the minimum score Emma can earn on her fifth and final test to pass?

A. 70%,

B. 62%

C. 55%

D. 50%

E. 42%

5) The width of a rectangle is $4x$, its length is $6x$, and its perimeter is 40. What is the value of x?

A. 1

B. 2

C. 4

D. 5

E. 6

6) In a classroom, there are y tables that can each seat 4 people and there are x tables that can each seat 7 people. What is the number of people that can be seated in the classroom?

A. $4y$

B. $7x$

C. $7x - 4y$

D. 13

E. $7x + 4y$

7) John has x dollars and he receives \$150. He then buys a bicycle that costs \$130. How much money does John have now?

A. $x + 150$

B. $x + 130$

C. $x + 20$

D. $x - 130$

E. $x - 20$

8) Jason is 15 miles ahead of Joe running at 5.5 miles per hour and Joe is running at the speed of 7 miles per hour. How long does it take Joe to catch Jason?

A. 3 *hours*

B. 4 *hours*

C. 6 *hours*

D. 8 *hours*

E. 10 *hours*

9) Five one – foot rulers can be split among how many users to leave each with $\frac{1}{5}$ of a ruler?

A. 4

B. 8

C. 25

D. 28

E. 30

10) The area of a circle is 49π. What is the diameter of the circle?

A. 4

B. 6

C. 12

D. 14

E. 16

11) The perimeter of a rectangular yard is 120 meters. What is its length if its width is twice its length?

A. 5 meters

B. 10 meters

C. 20 meters

D. 24 meters

E. 36 meters

12) A shirt costing $300 is discounted 20%. After a month, the shirt is discounted another 15%. Which of the following expressions can be used to find the selling price of the shirt?

A. (300) (0.70)

B. (300) − 300 (0.30)

C. (300)(0.20) − (300) (0.15)

D. (300) (0.80) (0.85)

E. (300)(0.80)(0.85) − (300) (0.15)

13) The average of 6 numbers is 14. The average of 4 of those numbers is 10. What is the average of the other two numbers?

A. 10

B. 12

C. 14

D. 22

E. 28

14) What is the value of x in this equation? $3x + 10 = 37$

A. 18

B. 16

C. 12

D. 9

E. 6

15) If $x + 4 = 8$, $2y - 3 = 5$ then $xy + 10 =$

A. 9

B. 19

C. 21

D. 26

E. 32

16) A card is drawn at random from a standard 52–card deck, what is the probability that the card is of Spades? (The deck includes 13 of each suit clubs, diamonds, hearts, and spades)

A. $\frac{1}{4}$

B. $\frac{1}{2}$

C. $\frac{1}{6}$

D. $\frac{1}{78}$

E. $\frac{1}{104}$

17) Which of the following is NOT less than $\frac{1}{5}$?

A. $\frac{1}{7}$

B. $\frac{1}{4}$

C. $\frac{1}{9}$

D. 10%

E. 0.18

18) Mr. Jones saves $2,500 out of his monthly family income of $75,000. What fractional part of his income does he save?

A. $\frac{1}{30}$

B. $\frac{1}{11}$

C. $\frac{3}{26}$

D. $\frac{4}{15}$

E. $\frac{1}{15}$

19) The mean of 50 test scores was calculated as 90. But it turned out that one of the scores was misread as 84 but it was 59. What is the mean?

A. 85

B. 88

C. 89.5

D. 90.2

E. 90.5

20) If $3x - 5 = 19$, then $2x + 6 =$?

A. 16

B. 20

C. 22

D. 24

E. 28

21) What is the equivalent temperature of $167°F$ in Celsius? ($C = Celsius$)

$$C = \frac{5}{9}(F - 32)$$

A. 32

B. 40

C. 48

D. 52

E. 75

22) The width of a box is one third of its length. The height of the box is half of its width. If the length of the box is $36cm$, what is the volume of the box?

A. $81 \ cm^3$

B. $165 cm^3$

C. $248 \ cm^3$

D. $768 \ cm^3$

E. $2,592 \ cm^3$

23) If 150% of a number is 45, then what is the 80% of that number?

A. 24

B. 45

C. 50

D. 85

E. 80

24) The perimeter of the trapezoid below is $46 \ cm$. What is its area?

A. $48 \ cm^2$

B. $70 \ cm^2$

C. $132 \ cm^2$

D. $576 \ cm^2$

E. $986 \ cm^2$

12 cm

5 cm

7cm

25) In two successive years, the population of a town is increased by 16% and 20%. What percent of the population is increased after two years?

A. 32%

B. 36%

C. 39%

D. 68%

E. 72%

SSAT Middle Level Math Practice Test 2

2023 - 2024

Two Parts

▶ **Total number of questions:** 50
▶ **Section 1:** 25 questions
▶ **Section 2:** 25 questions
▶ **Total time for two parts:** 60 Minutes

SSAT Middle Level Practice Tests Answer Sheet

Remove (or photocopy) these answer sheets and use them to complete the practice tests.

SSAT Middle Level Mathematics Practice Test Answer Sheet

SSAT Middle Level Math Section 1

1	Ⓐ Ⓑ Ⓒ Ⓓ Ⓔ	11	Ⓐ Ⓑ Ⓒ Ⓓ Ⓔ	21	Ⓐ Ⓑ Ⓒ Ⓓ Ⓔ
2	Ⓐ Ⓑ Ⓒ Ⓓ Ⓔ	12	Ⓐ Ⓑ Ⓒ Ⓓ Ⓔ	22	Ⓐ Ⓑ Ⓒ Ⓓ Ⓔ
3	Ⓐ Ⓑ Ⓒ Ⓓ Ⓔ	13	Ⓐ Ⓑ Ⓒ Ⓓ Ⓔ	23	Ⓐ Ⓑ Ⓒ Ⓓ Ⓔ
4	Ⓐ Ⓑ Ⓒ Ⓓ Ⓔ	14	Ⓐ Ⓑ Ⓒ Ⓓ Ⓔ	24	Ⓐ Ⓑ Ⓒ Ⓓ Ⓔ
5	Ⓐ Ⓑ Ⓒ Ⓓ Ⓔ	15	Ⓐ Ⓑ Ⓒ Ⓓ Ⓔ	25	Ⓐ Ⓑ Ⓒ Ⓓ Ⓔ
6	Ⓐ Ⓑ Ⓒ Ⓓ Ⓔ	16	Ⓐ Ⓑ Ⓒ Ⓓ Ⓔ		
7	Ⓐ Ⓑ Ⓒ Ⓓ Ⓔ	17	Ⓐ Ⓑ Ⓒ Ⓓ Ⓔ		
8	Ⓐ Ⓑ Ⓒ Ⓓ Ⓔ	18	Ⓐ Ⓑ Ⓒ Ⓓ Ⓔ		
9	Ⓐ Ⓑ Ⓒ Ⓓ Ⓔ	19	Ⓐ Ⓑ Ⓒ Ⓓ Ⓔ		
10	Ⓐ Ⓑ Ⓒ Ⓓ Ⓔ	20	Ⓐ Ⓑ Ⓒ Ⓓ Ⓔ		

SSAT Middle Level Math Section 2

1	Ⓐ Ⓑ Ⓒ Ⓓ Ⓔ	11	Ⓐ Ⓑ Ⓒ Ⓓ Ⓔ	21	Ⓐ Ⓑ Ⓒ Ⓓ Ⓔ
2	Ⓐ Ⓑ Ⓒ Ⓓ Ⓔ	12	Ⓐ Ⓑ Ⓒ Ⓓ Ⓔ	22	Ⓐ Ⓑ Ⓒ Ⓓ Ⓔ
3	Ⓐ Ⓑ Ⓒ Ⓓ Ⓔ	13	Ⓐ Ⓑ Ⓒ Ⓓ Ⓔ	23	Ⓐ Ⓑ Ⓒ Ⓓ Ⓔ
4	Ⓐ Ⓑ Ⓒ Ⓓ Ⓔ	14	Ⓐ Ⓑ Ⓒ Ⓓ Ⓔ	24	Ⓐ Ⓑ Ⓒ Ⓓ Ⓔ
5	Ⓐ Ⓑ Ⓒ Ⓓ Ⓔ	15	Ⓐ Ⓑ Ⓒ Ⓓ Ⓔ	25	Ⓐ Ⓑ Ⓒ Ⓓ Ⓔ
6	Ⓐ Ⓑ Ⓒ Ⓓ Ⓔ	16	Ⓐ Ⓑ Ⓒ Ⓓ Ⓔ		
7	Ⓐ Ⓑ Ⓒ Ⓓ Ⓔ	17	Ⓐ Ⓑ Ⓒ Ⓓ Ⓔ		
8	Ⓐ Ⓑ Ⓒ Ⓓ Ⓔ	18	Ⓐ Ⓑ Ⓒ Ⓓ Ⓔ		
9	Ⓐ Ⓑ Ⓒ Ⓓ Ⓔ	19	Ⓐ Ⓑ Ⓒ Ⓓ Ⓔ		
10	Ⓐ Ⓑ Ⓒ Ⓓ Ⓔ	20	Ⓐ Ⓑ Ⓒ Ⓓ Ⓔ		

SSAT Middle Level Math Practice Test 2 Section 1

Total number of questions: 25

Total time for this section: 30 Minutes

You may NOT use a calculator on this part.

1) If 15 percent of a number is 60, then 25 percent of the same number is ...

A. 65

B. 70

C. 80

D. 100

E. 120

2) Which of the following is NOT equal to 0.2×4?

A. 0.4×2

B. 1×0.8

C. $\frac{16}{8} \times \frac{4}{10}$

D. $\frac{5}{15} \times 3$

E. 0.8×1

3) Sara has N books. Mary has 5 more books than Sara. If Mary gives Sara 4 books, how many books will Mary have, in terms of N?

A. N

B. $N + 1$

C. $N + 2$

D. $N + 5$

E. $N - 5$

4) If $\frac{3x}{2} = 30$, then $\frac{2x}{5} = ?$

A. 8

B. 10

C. 15

D. 20

E. 40

5) Which of the following is closest to $\frac{1}{5}$ of 40?

A. 0.3×6

B. 0.3×5

C. 0.2×30

D. 0.2×35

E. 0.2×39.5

6) What is the area of a square whose diagonal is 6?

A. 18

B. 24

C. 36

D. 60

E. 64

7) An angle is equal to one eighth of its supplement. What is the measure of that angle?

A. 15

B. 20

C. 30

D. 45

E. 160

8) A $40 shirt now selling for $28 is discounted by what percent?

A. 20%

B. 30%

C. 40%

D. 60%

E. 80%

9) What is the value of x in the following figure? (Figure is not drawn to scale)

A. 150

B. 145

C. 125

D. 105

E. 85

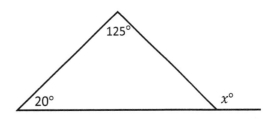

10) The perimeter of the trapezoid below is 54. What is its area?

A. $252cm^2$

B. $234\ cm^2$

C. $216\ cm^2$

D. $130\ cm^2$

E. $108\ cm^2$

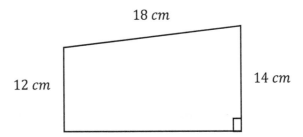

11) The score of Emma was half as that of Ava and the score of Mia was twice that of Ava. If the score of Mia was 60, what is the score of Emma?

A. 15

B. 18

C. 20

D. 30

E. 32

12) Two third of 30 is equal to $\frac{2}{5}$ of what number?

A. 15

B. 20

C. 30

D. 50

E. 60

13) If three times a number added to 6 equals to 30, what is the number?

A. 2

B. 4

C. 6

D. 8

E. 10

14) Solve for x: $4(x + 2) = 6(x - 4) + 20$

A. 12

B. 6

C. 5.5

D. 4

E. 2

15) Five years ago, Amy was three times as old as Mike was. If Mike is 10 years old now, how old is Amy?

A. 4

B. 8

C. 12

D. 15

E. 20

16) Two-kilograms apple and three-kilograms orange cost $26.4. If one-kilogram apple costs $4.2 how much does one-kilogram orange cost?

A. $9

B. $6

C. $5.5

D. $5

E. $4.5

17) The average weight of 18 girls in a class is 60 kg and the average weight of 32 boys in the same class is 62 kg. What is the average weight of all the 50 students in that class?

A. 61.28

B. 61.68

C. 61.90

D. 62.20

E. 64.00

18) What is the value of x in this equation? $6(x + 4) = 72$

A. 4

B. 6

C. 8

D. 10

E. 12

19) When a number is subtracted from 20 and the difference is divided by that number, the result is 3. What is the value of the number?

A. 2

B. 4

C. 5

D. 12

E. 15

20) Which of the following is the correct statement?

A. $\frac{3}{4} > 0.8$

B. $10\% = \frac{2}{5}$

C. $3 < \frac{5}{2}$

D. $\frac{5}{6} > 0.8$

E. $2.5\% = 0.25$

21) In a group of 5 books, the average number of pages is 24. Mary adds a book with 30 pages to the group. What is the new average number of pages per book?

A. 20

B. 22

C. 24

D. 25

E. 30

22) A football team won exactly 80% of the games it played during last session. Which of the following could be the total number of games the team played last season?

A. 49

B. 35

C. 32

D. 12

E. 8

23) If a gas tank can hold 25 gallons, how many gallons does it contain when it is $\frac{2}{5}$ full?

A. 50

B. 125

C. 62.5

D. 10

E. 8

24) A red box is 20% greater than a blue box. If 30 books exist in the red box, how many books are in the blue box?

A. 9

B. 15

C. 20

D. 25

E. 26

25)6 liters of water are poured into an aquarium that's 15 cm long, 5 cm wide, and 90 cm high. How many cm will the water level in the aquarium rise due to this added water? (1 $liter\ of\ water = 1,000\ cm^3$)

A. 80

B. 40

C. 20

D. 10

E. 8

IF YOU FINISH BEFORE TIME IS CALLED, YOU MAY CHECK YOUR WORK ON THIS SECTION ONLY. DO NOT TURN TO OTHER SECTION IN THE TEST.

STOP

.... www.EffortlessMath.com

SSAT Middle Level Math Practice Test 2 Section 2

Total number of questions: 25

Total time for this section: 30 Minutes

You may NOT use a calculator on this part.

1) A taxi driver earns $9 per 1-hour work. If he works 10 hours a day and in 1 hour he uses 2-liters petrol with price $1 for 1-liter. How much money does he earn in one day?

A. $90

B. $88

C. $70

D. $60

E. $56

2) Which of the following is less than $\frac{1}{5}$?

A. $\frac{1}{4}$

B. 0.5

C. $\frac{1}{6}$

D. 0.25

E. 0.3

3) Amy and John work in a same company. Last month, both of them received a raise of 20 percent. If Amy earns $30.00 *per hour* now and John earns $26.40, Amy earned how much more per hour than John before their raises?

A. $8.25

B. $4.25

C. $3.00

D. $2.25

E. $1.75

4) Four people can paint 4 houses in 10 days. How many people are needed to paint 8 houses in 5 days?

A. 6

B. 8

C. 12

D. 16

E. 20

5) If $N \times (5 - 3) = 12$ then $N =$?

A. 6

B. 12

C. 13

D. 14

E. 18

6) The length of a rectangle is 3 times of its width. If the length is 18, what is the perimeter of the rectangle?

A. 24

B. 30

C. 36

D. 48

E. 56

7) In the figure below, what is the value of x? (Figure is not drawn to scale)

A. 43

B. 67

C. 77

D. 90

E. 98

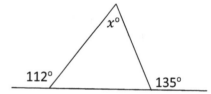

8) If $x \blacksquare y = 3x + y - 2$, what is the value of $4 \blacksquare 12$?

A. 4

B. 18

C. 22

D. 36

E. 48

9) The width of a rectangle is $4x$. the length is $6x$, and the perimeter of the rectangle is 80. What is the value of x?

A. 1

B. 2

C. 3

D. 4

E. 5

10) How many tiles of 8 cm^2 is needed to cover a floor of dimension 6 cm by 24 cm?

A. 6

B. 12

C. 18

D. 24

E. 30

11) If 0.45 equals $450M$, what is the value of M?

A. 0.0001

B. 0.001

C. 0.01

D. 1.00

E. 0.11

12) If $z = 3x + 6$, what does $2z + 3$ equal?

A. $6x + 6$

B. $6x + 12$

C. $6x - 12$

D. $6x - 6$

E. $6x + 15$

13) If 20 is the product of 2 and $2x$, then 20 is divisible by which of the following?

A. $x + 4$

B. $2x - 4$

C. $x - 2$

D. $x \times 4$

E. $x + 1$

$$0.ABC \qquad\qquad 0.0D$$

14) The letters represent two decimals listed above. One of the decimals is equivalent to $\frac{1}{8}$ and the other is equivalent to $\frac{1}{20}$. What is the product of C and D?

A. 0

B. 5

C. 25

D. 20

E. 40

15) $\frac{x}{x-3} = \frac{4}{5}$, $x - 5 =$?

A. -12

B. -15

C. -17

D. 12

E. 15

16) A company pays its employee $4,000 plus 2% of all sales profit. If x is the number of all sales profit, which of the following represents the employer's revenue?

A. $0.02x$

B. $0.98x - 4,000$

C. $0.02x + 4,000$

D. $0.98x + 4,000$

E. $0.2x + 4,000$

17) In a certain bookshelf of a library, there are 35 biology books, 95 history books, and 80 language books. What is the ratio of the number of biology books to the total number of books in this bookshelf?

A. $\frac{1}{4}$

B. $\frac{1}{6}$

C. $\frac{2}{7}$

D. $\frac{3}{8}$

E. $\frac{1}{4}$

18) If $6,000 + A - 200 = 7,400$, then $A = \cdots$

A. 200

B. 600

C. 1,600

D. 2,200

E. 3,000

19) The circle graph below shows all Mr. Taylor's expenses for last month. If he spent $660 on his car, how much did he spend for his rent?

A. $700

B. $740

C. $780

D. $810

E. $900

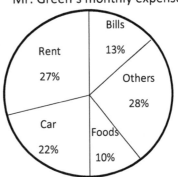

Mr. Green's monthly expenses

Bills 13%
Rent 27%
Others 28%
Car 22%
Foods 10%

20) If $5 \times M + 4 = 5$, M equals to ....

A. 2

B. 4

C. $\frac{1}{5}$

D. 6

E. $\frac{1}{3}$

21) Which of the following is equal to $\frac{42.6}{100}$?

A. 42.6

B. 4.26

C. 426.0

D. 0.0426

E. 0.426

22) In the following figure, point Q lies on line n, what is the value of y if $x = 35$? (Figure is not drawn to scale)

A. 15

B. 25

C. 35

D. 45

E. 60

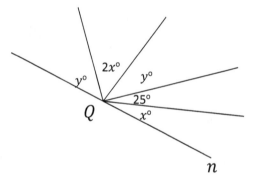

23) A container holds 3.5 gallons of water when it is $\frac{7}{24}$ full. How many gallons of water does the container hold when it's full?

A. 8

B. 12

C. 16

D. 20

E. 30

24) At a Zoo, the ratio of lions to tigers is 5 to 3. Which of the following could NOT be the total number of lions and tigers in the zoo?

A. 64

B. 80

C. 98

D. 104

E. 160

25) If x is greater than 48, then $\frac{1}{6}$ of x must be...

A. Greater than 12

B. Greater than 16

C. Equal to 16

D. Equal to 12

E. Less than 12

IF YOU FINISH BEFORE TIME IS CALLED, YOU MAY CHECK YOUR WORK ON THIS SECTION ONLY. DO NOT TURN TO ANY OTHER SECTION IN THE TEST. **STOP**

SSAT MIDDLE LEVEL MATH PRACTICE TESTS ANSWER KEYS

Now, it's time to review your results to see where you went wrong and what areas you need to improve.

SSAT Middle Level Math Practice Test 1								SSAT Middle Level Math Practice Test 2							
Section 1				Section 2				Section 1				Section 2			
1	B	16	E	1	E	16	A	1	D	16	B	1	C	16	C
2	C	17	C	2	E	17	B	2	D	17	A	2	C	17	B
3	B	18	C	3	C	18	A	3	B	18	C	3	C	18	C
4	A	19	E	4	B	19	C	4	A	19	C	4	D	19	D
5	B	20	D	5	B	20	C	5	E	20	D	5	A	20	C
6	C	21	A	6	E	21	E	6	A	21	D	6	D	21	E
7	E	22	E	7	C	22	E	7	B	22	B	7	B	22	B
8	C	23	A	8	E	23	A	8	B	23	D	8	C	23	B
9	D	24	C	9	C	24	C	9	B	24	D	9	D	24	C
10	E	25	E	10	D	25	C	10	D	25	A	10	C	25	A
11	C			11	C			11	A			11	B		
12	D			12	D			12	D			12	E		
13	B			13	D			13	D			13	D		
14	A			14	D			14	B			14	C		
15	A			15	D			15	E			15	C		

SSAT MIDDLE LEVEL MATH
PRACTICE TESTS
ANSWERS AND EXPLANATIONS

SSAT Middle Level Mathematics Practice Test 1
Section 1

1) Choice B is correct

30 percent of a number is 180. Therefore, the number is 600.

$0.30x = 180 \rightarrow x = \frac{180}{0.30} = 600$, 12 percent of 600 is 72. $0.12 \times 600 = 72$

1) Choice C is correct

0.45 equals $4.5F$. $0.45 = 4.5F \rightarrow F = \frac{0.45}{4.5} = 0.1$. Then: $10F = 10 \times 0.1 = 1$

2) Choice B is correct

Use simple interest formula: $I = prt$ (I = interest, p = principal, r = rate, t = time)

t is for one year. For 3 months, t is $\frac{1}{4}$ or 0.25, $I = (5,800)(0.04)(0.25) = 58$

3) Choice A is correct

Three times a certain number, increased by 6, is equal to 30. Write an equation and solve.

$$3x + 6 = 30 \rightarrow 3x = 30 - 6 = 24 \rightarrow x = \frac{24}{3} = 8$$

4) Choice B is correct

Use distance formula: $Distance = Rate \times time \Rightarrow 320 = 50 \times T$,

divide both sides by 50. $320 \div 50 = T \Rightarrow T = 6.4\ hours$.

Change hours to minutes for the decimal part. $0.4\ hours = 0.4 \times 60 = 24\ minutes$.

5) Choice C is correct

To find the discount, multiply the number by $(100\% - rate\ of\ discount)$.

Therefore, for the first discount we get: $(D)(100\% - 15\%) = (D)(0.85) = 0.85\ D$

For increase of 15%: $(0.85\ D)(100\% + 15\%) = (0.85\ D)(1.15) = 0.97\ D = 97\%\ of\ D$

6) Choice E is correct

$average = \frac{sum\ of\ terms}{number\ of\ terms} \Rightarrow 20 = \frac{14+16+21+x}{4} \Rightarrow 80 = 51 + x \Rightarrow x = 29$

7) Choice C is correct

$$\frac{x+4}{2} = 6 \rightarrow x + 4 = 2 \times 6 = 12 \rightarrow x = 12 - 4 = 8$$

8) Choice D is correct

John has M toy cars. Jack has 5 more cars than John. Therefore, Jack has $M + 5$ toy cars. Jack gives John 2 cars. Now, Jack has $(M + 5 - 2)$ $M + 3$ toy cars.

9) Choice E is correct

Write the equation and solve for B: $0.12A = 0.03B$, divide both sides by 0.03, then you will have $\frac{0.12}{0.03}A = B$, therefore: $B = 4A$, and B is 4 times of A or it's 400% of A.

10) Choice C is correct

The ratio of boy to girls is $3:2$. Therefore, there are 3 boys out of 5 students. To find the answer, first divide the total number of students by 5, then multiply the result by 3.

$$600 \div 5 = 120 \Rightarrow 120 \times 3 = 360$$

11) Choice D is correct

Add the first 5 numbers. $41 + 46 + 52 + 36 + 51 = 226$

To find the distance traveled in the next 5 hours, multiply the average by number of hours.

$Distance = Average \times Rate = 60 \times 5 = 300$, Add both numbers. $300 + 226 = 526$

12) Choice B is correct

Let x be the number. Write the equation and solve for x. $\frac{2}{3} \times 45 = \frac{4}{5} \times x \Rightarrow \frac{2 \times 45}{3} = \frac{4x}{5}$, use cross multiplication to solve for x. $5 \times 90 = 4x \times 3 \Rightarrow 450 = 12x \Rightarrow x = 37.5$

13) Choice A is correct

One pound of cheese costs $0.80. *One pound* $= 16$ *ounces*, 16 ounces of cheese costs $0.87. Then, 1 ounce of chees costs $(0.87 \div 16)$ $0.05. 6 ounces of cheese costs $(6 \times \$0.05)$ $0.30.

14) Choice A is correct

The percent of girls playing tennis is: $30\% \times 20\% = 0.30 \times 0.20 = 0.06 = 6\%$

15) Choice E is correct

$\frac{414}{600} = 0.69 = 69\%$. So, the discount is 31%.

16) Choice C is correct

Let x be the number. Write the equation and solve for x. $(36 - x) \div x = 3$, Multiply both sides by x. $(36 - x) = 3x$, then add x both sides. $36 = 4x$, now divide both sides by 4. $x = 9$

17) Choice C is correct

The failing rate is 12 out of $55 = \frac{12}{50}$, Change the fraction to percent: $\frac{12}{50} \times 100\% = 24\%$

24 percent of students failed. Therefore, 76 percent of students passed the exam.

18) Choice E is correct

$3x + 10 = 46 \rightarrow 3x = 46 - 10 = 36 \rightarrow x = \frac{36}{3} = 12$

19) Choice D is correct

If 18 balls are removed from the bag at random, there will be one ball in the bag. The probability of choosing a brown ball is 1 out of 19. Therefore, the probability of not choosing a brown ball is 18 out of 19 and the probability of having not a brown ball after removing 18 balls is the same.

20) Choice A is correct

$M \times \frac{4}{3} \times 4 = 1$, then $M \times \frac{16}{3} = 1$. Multiply both sides by $\frac{3}{16}$. $M \times \frac{16}{3} \times \frac{3}{16} = 1 \times \frac{3}{16} \rightarrow \frac{3 \times 16}{3 \times 16} M = \frac{3}{16} \rightarrow M = \frac{3}{16}$

21) Choice E is correct

$4.50 is what percent of $30? $4.5 \div 30 = 0.15 = 15\%$

22) Choice A is correct

Let x be the number of years. Therefore, $3,000 per year equals $3000x$. starting from $25,000 annual salary means you should add that amount to $3000x$. Income more than that is:

$I > 3,000x + 25,000$

23) Choice C is correct

Let x be the number. Write the equation and solve for x. $50\% \ of \ x = 5 \Rightarrow 0.5x = 5 \Rightarrow$

$x = 5 \div 0.50 = 10$

24) Choice E is correct

$\frac{z}{5} = 4 \rightarrow z = 4 \times 5 = 20$, $z + 5 = 20 + 5 = 25$

SSAT MIDDLE LEVEL MATHEMATICS PRACTICE TEST 1
SECTION 2

1) Choice E is correct

$(10 - 5) \times 4 = 10 + \square$

Then: $5 \times 4 = 10 + \square$, $20 = 10 + \square$, then $\square = 10$

2) Choice E is correct

$\frac{x - 3}{5} + 5 = 20 \rightarrow \frac{x - 3}{5} = 20 - 5 = 15 \rightarrow x - 3 = 15 \times 5 = 75 \rightarrow$

$x = 75 + 3 = 78$

3) Choice C is correct

Use simple interest formula: $I = prt$ ($I = $ interest, $p = $ principal, $r = $ rate, $t = $ time)

$I = (7,000)(0.055)(5) = 1,925$

4) Choice B is correct

Emma needs an 75% average to pass for five exams. Therefore, the sum of 5 exams must be at least $5 \times 75 = 375$, the sum of 4 exams is: $68 + 75 + 80 + 90 = 313$.

The minimum score Emma can earn on her fifth and final test to pass is: $375 - 313 = 62$

5) Choice B is correct

The width of a rectangle is $4x$ and its length is $6x$. Then, the perimeter of the rectangle is $20x$.

$Perimeter\ of\ a\ rectangle = 2(width + length) = 2(4x + 6x) = 20x$

The perimeter of the rectangle is 40. Then: $20x = 40 \rightarrow x = 2$

6) Choice E is correct

There are y tables that can each seat 4 people and there are x tables that can each seat 7 people. Therefore, $4y + 7x$ people can be seated in the classroom.

7) Choice C is correct

John has x dollars and he receives $150. Therefore, he has $x + 150$. He then buys a bicycle that costs $130. Now, he has: $x + 150 - 130 = x + 20$

8) Choice E is correct

The distance between Jason and Joe is 15 miles. Jason running at 5.5 miles per hour and Joe is running at the speed of 7 miles per hour. Therefore, every hour the distance is 1.5 miles less. $15 \div 1.5 = 10$

9) Choice C is correct

$5 \div \frac{1}{5} = 25$

10) Choice D is correct

The formula for the area of the circle is: $= \pi r^2$, The area of the circle is 49π. Therefore:

$A = \pi r^2 \Rightarrow 49\pi = \pi r^2$, **Divide both sides by π: $49 = r^2 \Rightarrow r = 7$**

Diameter of a circle is $2 \times$ radius. Then: Diameter $= 2 \times 7 = 14$

11) Choice C is correct

The width of the rectangle is twice its length. Let x be the length. Then, $width = 2x$, Perimeter of the rectangle is $2\ (width + length) = 2(2x + x) = 120 \Rightarrow 6x = 120 \Rightarrow x = 20$

Length of the rectangle is 20 meters.

12) Choice D is correct

To find the discount, multiply the number by $(100\% - rate\ of\ discount)$.

Therefore, for the first discount we get: $(300)\ (100\% - 20\%) = (300)\ (0.80)$

For the next 15% discount: $(300)\ (0.80)\ (0.85)$

13) Choice D is correct

$average = \frac{sum\ of\ terms}{number\ of\ terms} \Rightarrow$ (average of 6 numbers) $14 = \frac{sum\ of\ numbers}{6} \Rightarrow$ sum of 6 numbers is : $14 \times 6 = 84$.

(average of 4 numbers) $10 = \frac{sum\ of\ numbers}{4} \Rightarrow$ sum of 4 numbers is $10 \times 4 = 40$

$sum\ of\ 6\ numbers - sum\ of\ 4\ numbers = sum\ of\ 2\ numbers$

$84 - 40 = 44$ average of 2 numbers $= \frac{44}{2} = 22$

14) Choice D is correct

$3x + 10 = 37 \rightarrow 3x = 37 - 10 = 27 \rightarrow x = \dfrac{27}{3} = 9$

15) Choice D is correct

$x + 4 = 8 \rightarrow x = 8 - 4 = 4, \ 2y - 3 = 5 \rightarrow 2y = 8 \rightarrow y = 4, \quad xy + 10 = 4 \times 4 + 10 = 26$

16) Choice A is correct

The deck contains 13 Spades. Then, the probability of choosing a Spades is $\dfrac{13}{52} = \dfrac{1}{4}$

17) Choice B is correct

From the choices provided, only $\dfrac{1}{4}$ is greater than $\dfrac{1}{5}$.

18) Choice A is correct

2,500 out of 75,000 equals to $\dfrac{2,500}{75,000} = \dfrac{25}{750} = \dfrac{1}{30}$

19) Choice C is correct

$$average \ (mean) = \frac{sum \ of \ terms}{number \ of \ terms} \Rightarrow 90 = \frac{sum \ of \ terms}{50} \Rightarrow sum = 90 \times 50 = 4,500$$

The difference of 84 and 59 is 25. Therefore, 25 should be subtracted from the sum.

$4,500 - 25 = 4,475, \ mean = \dfrac{sum \ of \ terms}{number \ of \ terms} \Rightarrow mean = \dfrac{4,475}{50} = 89.5$

20) Choice C is correct

$3x - 5 = 19 \Rightarrow 3x = 24 \Rightarrow x = 8$, then $2x + 6 = 2 \times 8 + 6 = 16 + 6 = 22$

21) Choice E is correct

Plug in 167 for F and then solve for C.

$C = \dfrac{5}{9} (F - 32) \Rightarrow C = \dfrac{5}{9} (167 - 32) \Rightarrow C = \dfrac{5}{9} (135) = 75$

22) Choice E is correct

If the length of the box is 36, then the width of the box is one third of it, 12, and the height of the box is 6(half of the width). The volume of the box is:

$Volume \ of \ a \ box = (length) \times (width) \times (height) = (36) \times (12) \times (6) = 2,592$

23) Choice A is correct

First, find the number. Let x be the number. Write the equation and solve for x. 150% of a number is 45, then: $1.5 \times x = 45 \Rightarrow x = 45 \div 1.5 = 30$, 80% of 30 is: $0.8 \times 30 = 24$

24) Choice C is correct

The perimeter of the trapezoid is 46. Therefore, the missing side (height) is $=$ $46 - 7 - 12 - 5 = 22$. Area of a trapezoid: $A = \frac{1}{2} h (b_1 + b_2) = \frac{1}{2} (22) (5 + 7) = 132$

25) Choice C is correct

the population is increased by 16% and 20%. 16% increase changes the population to 116% of original population. For the second increase, multiply the result by 120%.

$(1.16) \times (1.20) = 1.39 = 139\%$, 39 percent of the population is increased after two years.

SSAT Middle Level Mathematics Practice Test 2
Section 1

1) Choice D is correct

If 15 percent of a number is 60, then the number is: $15\% \; of \; x = 60 \rightarrow 0.15x = 60 \rightarrow x = \frac{60}{0.15} = 400$, 25 percent of 400 is: $25\% \; of \; 200 = \frac{25}{100} \times 400 = 100$

2) Choice D is correct

$0.2 \times 4 = 0.8$, all **choices** provided are equal to 0.8 except choice D. $\frac{5}{15} \times 3 = 1$

3) Choice B is correct

Sara has N books. Mary has 5 more books than Sara. Then, Mary has $N + 5$ books. If Mary gives Sara 4 books, Mary will have: $N + 5 - 4 = N + 1$

4) Choice A is correct

If $\frac{3x}{2} = 30$, then $3x = 60 \rightarrow x = 20$, $\frac{2x}{5} = \frac{2 \times 20}{5} = \frac{40}{5} = 8$

5) Choice E is correct

$\frac{1}{5}$ of 40 is 8. Let's review the **choices** provided:

A. $0.3 \times 6 = 1.8$

B. $0.3 \times 5 = 1.5$

C. $0.2 \times 30 = 6$

D. $0.2 \times 35 = 7$

E. $0.2 \times 39.5 = 7.9$

Option E is the closest to 8.

6) Choice A is correct

The diagonal of the square is 6. Let x be the side.

Use Pythagorean Theorem: $a^2 + b^2 = c^2$

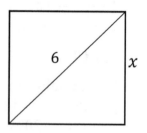

$x^2 + x^2 = 6^2 \Rightarrow 2x^2 = 6^2 \Rightarrow 2x^2 = 36 \Rightarrow x^2 = 18 \Rightarrow x = \sqrt{18}$

The area of the square is: $\sqrt{18} \times \sqrt{18} = 18$

7) Choice B is correct

The sum of supplement angles is 180. Let x be that angle. Therefore, $x + 8x = 180$

$9x = 180$, divide both sides by 9: $x = 20$

8) Choice B is correct

Use the formula for Percent of Change: $\dfrac{New\ Value - Old\ Value}{Old\ Value} \times 100\%$

$\dfrac{28-40}{40} \times 100\% = -30\%$ (negative sign here means that the new price is less than old price)

9) Choice B is correct

$x = 20 + 125 = 145$

10) Choice D is correct

The perimeter of the trapezoid is 54.

Therefore, the missing side (height) is $= 54 - 18 - 12 - 14 = 10$

Area of the trapezoid: $A = \frac{1}{2} h (b_1 + b_2) = \frac{1}{2} (10)(12 + 14) = 130$

11) Choice A is correct

If the score of Mia was 60, therefore the score of Ava is 30. Since, the score of Emma was half as that of Ava, therefore, the score of Emma is 15.

12) Choice D is correct

Let x be the number. Write the equation and solve for x.

$\frac{2}{3} \times 30 = \frac{2}{5} \times x \Rightarrow \frac{2 \times 30}{3} = \frac{2x}{5}$, use cross multiplication to solve for x.

$5 \times 60 = 2x \times 3 \Rightarrow 300 = 6x \Rightarrow x = 50$

13) Choice D is correct

Let x be the number. Then: $3x + 6 = 30$, Solve for x: $3x + 6 = 30 \rightarrow 3x = 30 - 6 = 24 \rightarrow x = 24 \div 3 = 8$

14) Choice B is correct

Simplify and solve for x in the equation. $4(x + 2) = 6(x - 4) + 20 \rightarrow 4x + 8 = 6x - 24 + 20$

$4x + 8 = 6x - 4$, Subtract $4x$ from both sides: $8 = 2x - 4$, Add 4 to both sides: $12 = 2x, 6 = x$

15) Choice E is correct

Five years ago, Amy was three times as old as Mike. Mike is 10 years now. Therefore, 5 years ago Mike was 5 years. Five years ago, Amy was: $A = 3 \times 5 = 15$

Now Amy is 20 years old: $15 + 5 = 20$

16) Choice B is correct

Let x be one-kilogram orange cost, then: $3x + (2 \times 4.2) = 26.4 \rightarrow$ $3x + 8.4 = 26.4 \rightarrow 3x = 26.4 - 8.4 \rightarrow 3x = 18 \rightarrow x = \frac{18}{3} = \$6$

17) Choice A is correct

$average = \frac{sum\ of\ terms}{number\ of\ terms}$, The sum of the weight of all girls is: $18 \times 60 = 1080\ kg$, The sum of the weight of all boys is: $32 \times 62 = 1984\ kg$, The sum of the weight of all students is: $1,080 + 1,984 = 3,064\ kg$, $Average = \frac{3064}{50} = 61.28$

18) Choice C is correct

Solve for x in the equation. $6(x + 4) = 72 \rightarrow 6x + 24 = 72 \rightarrow 6x = 72 - 24 = 48 \rightarrow x = 48 \div 6 = 8$

19) Choice C is correct

Let x be the number. Write the equation and solve for x. $(20 - x) \div x = 3$

Multiply both sides by x. $(20 - x) = 3x$, then add x both sides. $20 = 4x$, now divide both sides by 4. $x = 5$

20) Choice D is correct

Only option D is correct. $\frac{5}{6} = 0.83 \rightarrow 0.8 < \frac{5}{6}$

21) Choice D is correct

In a group of 5 books, the average number of pages is 24. Therefore, the sum of pages in all 5 books is $(5 \times 24 = 120)$. Mary adds a book with 30 pages to the group. Then, the sum of pages in all 6 books is $(5 \times 24 + 30 = 150)$. The new average number of pages per book is: $\frac{150}{6} = 25$

22) Choice B is correct

Choices A, C, D, and E are incorrect because 80% of each of the numbers is a non-whole number.

A. 49 $80\% \ of \ 49 \ = \ 0.80 \times 49 = 39.2$

B. 35 $80\% \ of \ 35 = 0.80 \times 35 = 28$

C. 32 $80\% \ of \ 32 = 0.80 \times 32 = 25.6$

D. 12 $80\% \ of \ 12 = 0.80 \times 12 = 9.6$

E. $880\% \ of \ 8 = 0.80 \times 8 = 6.4$

23) Choice D is correct

$\frac{2}{5} \times 25 = \frac{50}{5} = 10$

24) Choice D is correct

The red box is 20% greater than the blue box. Let x be the capacity of the blue box. Then:

$$x + 20\% \ of \ x = 30 \rightarrow 1.2x = 30 \rightarrow x = \frac{30}{1.2} = 25$$

25) Choice A is correct

$One \ liter = 1,000 \ cm^3 \rightarrow 6 \ liters = 6,000 \ cm^3$. Let's put h for the height of the water. Then:

$6,000 = 15 \times 5 \times h \rightarrow h = \frac{6,000}{75} = 80 \ cm$

SSAT Middle Level Mathematics Practice Test 2
Section 2

1) Choice C is correct

$9 \times 10 = \$90$, Petrol use: $10 \times 2 = 20$ liters, Petrol cost: $20 \times \$1 = \$20$

Money earned: $\$90 - \$20 = \$70$

2) Choice C is correct

From the **choices** provided, only C $(\frac{1}{6})$ is less than $\frac{1}{5}$.

3) Choice C is correct

Amy earns $30.00 *per hour* now. $30.00 *per hour* is 20 percent more than her previous rate. Let x be her rate before her raise. Then: $x + 0.20x = 30 \rightarrow 1.2x = 30 \rightarrow x = \frac{30}{1.2} = 25$

John earns $26.40 *per hour* now. $26.40 *per hour* is 20 percent more than his previous rate. Let x be John's rate before his raise. Then: $x + 0.20x = 26.40 \rightarrow 1.2x = 26.40 \rightarrow x = \frac{26.40}{1.2} = 22$, Amy earned $3.00 more per hour than John before their raises.

4) Choice D is correct.

Four people can paint 4 houses in 10 days. It means that for painting 8 houses in 10 days we need 8 people. To paint 8 houses in 5 days, 16 people are needed.

5) Choice A is correct.

$N \times (5 - 3) = 12 \rightarrow N \times 2 = 12 \rightarrow N = 6$

6) Choice D is correct.

The length of the rectangle is 18. Then, its width is 6. $18 \div 3 = 6$

$Perimeter\ of\ a\ rectangle = 2 \times width + 2 \times length = 2 \times 6 + 2 \times 18 = 12 + 36 = 48$

7) Choice B is correct

$\alpha = 180° - 112° = 68°$, $b = 180° - 135° = 45°$, The sum of all angles in a triangle is 180 degrees. Then: $x + \alpha + b = 180° \rightarrow x = 180° - 68° - 45° = 67°$

8) Choice C is correct.

If $x \blacksquare y = 3x + y - 2$, Then: $4 \blacksquare 12 = 3(4) + 12 - 2 = 12 + 12 - 2 = 22$

9) Choice D is correct

The width of a rectangle is $4x$ and its length is $6x$. Therefore, the perimeter of the rectangle is $20x$. *Perimeter of a rectangle* $= 2(width + length) = 2(4x + 6x) = 2(10x) = 20x$

The perimeter of the rectangle is 80. Then: $20x = 80 \rightarrow x = 4$

10) Choice C is correct

The area of the floor is: $6\ cm \times 24\ cm = 144\ cm^2$, The number is tiles needed $= 144 \div 8 = 18$

11) Choice B is correct

0.45 equals $450M$. Then: $450M = 0.45 \rightarrow M = \frac{0.45}{450} = 0.001$

12) Choice E is correct

$z = 3x + 6$, then, $2z = 2(3x + 6) = 6x + 12$, $2z + 3 = 6x + 12 + 3 = 6x + 15$

13) Choice D is correct.

$20 = 2x \times 2 \rightarrow x = 20 \div 4 = 5$

x equals to 5. Let's review the **choices** provided:

A. $x + 4 \rightarrow 5 + 4 = 9$ 20 is not divisible by 9.

B. $2x - 4 \rightarrow 2 \times 5 - 4 = 6$ 20 is not divisible by 6.

C. $x - 2 \rightarrow 5 - 2 = 3$ 20 is not divisible by 3.

D. $x \times 4 \rightarrow 5 \times 4 = 20$ 20 is divisible by 20.

E. $x + 1 \rightarrow 5 + 1 = 6$ 20 is not divisible by 6.

The answer is D.

14) Choice C is correct

$\frac{1}{8} = 0.125 \rightarrow C = 5$, $\frac{1}{20} = 0.05 \rightarrow D = 5 \rightarrow C \times D = 5 \times 5 = 25$

15) Choice C is correct

Use cross product to solve for x. $\frac{x}{x-3} = \frac{4}{5} \rightarrow 5 \times x = 4 \times (x - 3) \rightarrow 5x = 4x - 12 \rightarrow x = -12$

$\rightarrow x - 5 = -12 - 5 = -17$

16) Choice C is correct

x is the number of all sales profit and 2% of it is: $2\% \times x = 0.02x$, Employee's revenue:

$0.02x + 4,000$

17) Choice B is correct

Number of biology book: 35, total number of books; $35 + 95 + 80 = 210$

the ratio of the number of biology books to the total number of books is: $\frac{35}{210} = \frac{1}{6}$

18) Choice C is correct.

$6,000 + A - 200 = 7,400 \rightarrow 6,000 + A = 7,400 + 200 = 7,600 \rightarrow A = 7,600 - 6,000 = 1,600$

19) Choice D is correct

Let x be all expenses, then $\frac{22}{100}x = \$660 \rightarrow x = \frac{100 \times \$660}{22} = \$3,000$

Mr. Jones spent for his rent: $\frac{27}{100} \times \$3,000 = \$810$

20) Choice C is correct

$5 \times M + 4 = 5 \rightarrow 5 \times M = 5 - 4 = 1 \rightarrow M = \frac{1}{5}$

21) Choice E is correct

$\frac{42.6}{100} = 0.426$

22) Choice B is correct

The angles on a straight line add up to 180 degrees. Then: $x + 25 + y + 2x + y = 180$

Then, $3x + 2y = 180 - 25 \rightarrow 3(35) + 2y = 155, \rightarrow 2y = 155 - 105 = 50 \rightarrow y = 25$

23) Choice B is correct

let x be the number of gallons of water the container holds when it is full.

Then; $\frac{7}{24}x = 3.5 \rightarrow x = \frac{24 \times 3.5}{7} = 12$

24) Choice C is correct.

The ratio of lions to tigers is 5 to 3 at the zoo. Therefore, total number of lions and tigers must be divisible by 8. $5 + 3 = 8$, From the numbers provided, only 98 is not divisible by 8.

25) Choice A is correct

If x is greater than 18, then $\frac{1}{6}$ of x must be greater than: $\frac{1}{6} \times 18 = 3$.

"Effortless Math Education" Publications

Effortless Math authors' team strives to prepare and publish the best quality SSAT Middle Level Mathematics learning resources to make learning Math easier for all. We hope that our publications help you learn Math in an effective way and prepare for the SSAT Middle Level test.

We all in Effortless Math wish you good luck and successful studies!

Effortless Math Authors

www.EffortlessMath.com

... So Much More Online!

❖ FREE Math lessons

❖ More Math learning books!

❖ Mathematics Worksheets

❖ Online Math Tutors

Need a PDF version of this book?

Visit www.EffortlessMath.com

Receive the PDF version of this book or get another FREE book!

Thank you for using our Book!

Do you LOVE this book?

Then, you can get the PDF version of this book or another book absolutely FREE!

Please email us at:

info@EffortlessMath.com

for details.

Printed in the USA
CPSIA information can be obtained
at www.ICGtesting.com
LVHW060828210823
755770LV00006B/381

9 781646 128